STAIRWAY
to
AWESOMENESS!

30 Fundamental Steps to Living a Life of Awesomeness

Kim! Stay HIGH on AWESOMENESS so reality cannot destroy you! Tanya aka Comic Strip Mama!

COMIC STRIP MAMA
aka Tanya Masse

Stairway to Awesomeness!

Copyright © 2013 by Comic Strip Mama Enterprises Inc. aka Tanya Masse.

All Rights Reserved.

No part of this publication may be reproduced, stored in a retrieval system, or transmitted, in any form or by any means, electronic, mechanical, photocopying, recording, or otherwise, without prior written permission from the author.

This is a work of fiction. Names, characters, places and incidents either are the product of the author's imagination or are used fictitiously. And any resemblance to actual persons, living, dead (or in any other form), business establishments, events, or locales is entirely coincidental.

www.comicstripmama.com

FIRST EDITION TRADE PAPERBACK

Imajin Books

August 15, 2013

ISBN: 978-1-927792-19-3

Cover designed by Tanya Masse and Ryan Doan.
www.ryandoan.com

Interior graphics by Comic Strip Mama Enterprises Inc./Tanya Masse

Praise for Stairway to Awesomeness

"I just finished reading *Stairway to Awesomeness* and Comic Strip Mama has opened my heart and my eyes to a brand new way of looking at life! She is absolutely right when she says, life is too short, to take things way too seriously! I believe that if everyone practiced the simple steps outlined in her book, this world would be a brighter place! Her spirit shines through even during her darkest moments. She has inspired me to start embracing all that is good in this world and to find the joy in everyday life even when it seems like the impossible! I will no longer settle for anything less than a life filled with awesomeness!!! Thank you, Comic Strip Mama, for showing us that with a little bit of effort, it can be done! You are a wonderful teacher and inspiration to us all!" —Carolyn Coppola, author of *Minivans, Meltdowns & Merlot*

"*Stairway to Awesomeness* is like having a witty, wise aunt there for you during the bumpy times in life, who wipes away tears while serving a cup of hot cocoa and making you laugh so hard your sides hurt. Comic Strip Mama uses humor to point out some of the most common mistakes people make in the way we view the world any time we think, "My personality is me and my attitude depends on you." This is the perfect book for every parent to keep in their own time-out room...to flip through, find any one of a number of sanity-saving illustrations, and regain a grip on setting a better example than the previous generation. Highly recommended!" —Cynthia Sue Larson, bestselling author of *Reality Shifts*

"*Stairway to Awesomeness* by Tanya Masse is an inspiring, motivating and enjoyable read. Its premise is that anyone, with the right attitude, can not only overcome any challenge that life throws at them, but can thrive through adversity. Tanya uses her own life as an example of awesomeness in action as she takes readers through her early years that were rife with tragedy. Any one event from those times could have turned her into a bitter, angry person but her sense of positivity kept her moving forward until the day she realized that she could shape her own destiny through the choices and attitudes she adopts. Tanya, also known as 'Comic Strip Mama,' uses life stories, self-reflection, honesty, and humorous cartoons to illustrate her position that life is (dare I say it?) awesome. Her subject matter could easily devolve into platitudes, but Tanya is much better than that. She accepts – and recommends that readers accept – that no one is 'perfect' and that trying to be so simply sets oneself up for failure and misery. Rather, she recommends that we stop trying so hard all the time, that we laugh as much as possible (even at ourselves), that we live our lives with the understanding that what goes around comes around (karma), and that we trade in a sense of entitlement for a sense of gratitude. *Stairway to Awesomeness* will make you smile and laugh as you meet yourself in its pages. A kinder, gentler you, perhaps, but the "you" you should really allow yourself to be." — Katherine Mariaca-Sullivan, author of *The Complication of Sisters*

"What a zany, quirky, addictive go-to book. I really enjoyed reading this. Best of luck, Tanya, on this novel approach to happiness." —Dr. Neal Houston, The Life Therapy Group

"Life changing. Truly. Tanya uses her naked candor and refreshing humor to relay her tried-and-true life lessons in an entertaining and inspiring way. Her shocking, yet somehow relatable, life story proves that if she has figured out a way to be happy, the rest of us don't really have an excuse. Here's to awesomeness!" —Nicole Coon, Rachel Morrow and Jennifer Quinn, authors of *Not Your Ordinary Parenting Book: Newborn Edition: 101 Tricks That Take the Guesswork out of Parenting*

Table of Contents

A little Message from Mama: 1
My Intention and a Little Disclaimer 2
Allow ME to Introduce MYSELF! 4
My Childhood Years 5
My Teen Years 8
Adulthood (A little sooner than it had to be) 10
The Steps 16
#1 – Life is Hard. Expect it to BE! 17
#2 – Embrace the INSANITY! 20
#3 – Get Over YOURSELF! 23
#4 – Give Yourself an ATTITUDE Adjustment! 27
#5 – LEARN Who YOU Really Are! 35
#6 – Discover Your Purpose! 39
#7 – Make Peace With Your Past! 46
#8 – Accept Accountability! 51
#9 – Stop Setting Yourself Up for FAILURE! 55
#10 – Try Not to Assume! 65
#11 – Release Anger, Negativity & Toxic Drama! 68
#12 – Get Over Your False Sense of ENTITLEMENT! 77
#13 – Live SIMPLY Within Your Means! 81
#14 – Don't Succumb to Your Weaknesses & Fears! 85
#15 – Surround Yourself With People Who Bring Out the BEST in YOU! 89
#16 – Make Good LIFE Investments! 94
#17 – Get ON That BUCKET LIST! 98
#18 – Embrace Life Changes! 104
#19 – Open Your MIND! 111
#20 – STOP Taking Life WAY Too Seriously!!! 114
#21 – Respect and Accept Differences! 121
#22 – Don't Measure Success in Dollars & Cents! 125

#23 – Take Time for Yourself, Take Care of Yourself & Reward Yourself! .. 128
#24 – Do Random Acts of Awesomeness! 132
#25 – Give Yourself Regular Reality Checks! 136
#26 – Believe in Something LARGER than LIFE! 139
#27 – Enjoy Life, Have Fun and Socialize MORE! 143
#28 – Make the MOST of EVERY MOMENT! 146
#29 – Find the Positive Lessons, the Blessings & the Humor in Adversity! ... 149
#30 – BE an AWESOME Role Model! 155
THANK YOU & Conclusion 159
Some Acknowledgements of the STUFF That Makes it WORTHWHILE! 161
Allow ME to Introduce the Comic Cast! 164
Just Comics! 168
Dedications & Special Mentions! 192
About the Author 195

A little Message from Mama:

To me, "Awesomeness" is the closest thing to perfection that a human being can possibly achieve. Awesomeness encompasses so much that I will talk about in this book, but most importantly, it encompasses strength, happiness, success, purpose and self-worth — all of the things we so desperately seek throughout our journey of life. It is the ultimate feeling of being complete and living life to the absolute fullest.

The key to achieving true awesomeness is recognizing it, wanting it, pursuing it and practicing it, even in the face of adversity and tragedy!

Anyone can just EXIST... BUT, being AWESOME takes PRACTICE!

©2013 Comic Strip Mama Enterprises Inc.

My Intention and a Little Disclaimer

My real life name is Tanya and many of you probably know me as the Comic Strip Mama! Well, in this book I'm not speaking to you as a parent. The things that you will learn from this book will certainly and ultimately help you be a better parent, but that is not what this book is about. This book is all about learning how to change your way of thinking, how to embrace the insanity of life and how to be an awesome, strong, happy and positive person. My next book will be ALL about "the awesome, the insanity and the drama" of parenthood, but for now, what you have in your hands is all about YOU!

Anybody who really knows me as the person I am today will probably tell you that I am a strong, happy, positive, loving, kind and a little bit insane woman and mother with a witty sense of humor who NEVER takes life very seriously and who always looks for the awesome in every person and everything. *BIG deep breath* Cuz that was a really loooong sentence!

Well it's true. That is exactly who I am today. And if I can't manage to somehow find the awesome or at least the good in someone or something, I will look for the blessings, the positive lessons and the funny. It's just what I do. And that's why I love being a comic strip artist and writer!

My "Comic Strip Mama" venture all started with the simple notion that I was determined to encourage others to focus the positive and the humor while struggling through the insanity and challenges of life and parenthood instead of taking it WAY too seriously. And I'm thrilled that I'm actually doing it! If you think about it, a lot of the negativity in the world today exists simply because people CHOOSE to take life way too seriously and that really needs to change.

The truth is I was not always this awesome, strong, happy and positive person...I had to lose a lot, struggle a lot and learn to BE this way. I will never stop living and learning and I still struggle some days, but that's ok. I know exactly what I have to do to KEEP BEING this way and that is why I'm writing this book. It is my hope that I will help others learn how to BE the same way simply because it's an awesome way to live and be. And if more people are living life being awesome and happy, think about how awesome and happy the entire world would be!

AWESOME
Happiness
Strength
Positivity
Blessings
Humor
CHOICES
Depression
Negativity
Anger
Self-Pity
Toxic Drama
NOT AWESOME
I'm going this way!
Me TOO!

Allow ME to Introduce MYSELF!

I know, I know. I'm probably not going to change the world. But I will make an honest effort to try.

Now let me make something perfectly clear, I am not a therapist, a psychologist, a doctor of any sort or an educated mental health professional with any type of degree or designation. My "credentials" do not come from reading and studying text books, passing exams or graduating with a diploma. They were earned the hard way, the real way, through a lot of hardcore living and learning. That being said, I am extremely confident that I have nailed down the essential fundamentals of living a happy, positive and awesome life.

Also, you should know that I am not writing this book because I think that I have lived the toughest life EVER. I know that others have felt worse, seen worse and lived through much worse. I am thankful every day that I don't live in war, or in a "third world". I am thankful that I have my rights and freedoms as a woman and citizen of my country. I am SO grateful for so many things despite the fact that I have not had the easiest life. However, I also recognize that just because bad things happen, it doesn't mean you have to live a negative and miserable existence.

The intention of writing this book is NOT to make you feel sorry for me in any way whatsoever. My intention is simply to share what I have lived, what I have learned and how I have changed my way of thinking and being in an effort to help you realize that awesomeness CAN be achieved despite the adversity you face in this life. I also want to prove to you that there are blessings and positive lessons to be found in everything, even tragic things. Whether you choose to recognize them, or not, is YOUR choice.

My Childhood Years

My childhood was bittersweet. I remember being very loved especially by my extended family, but I also remember being very scared and lost. In all honesty, my parents were not the best of parents. I'd like to believe that the reasoning was simply because they were not ready to be parents, so they were a little selfish and therefore made some really bad choices.

First, I will tell you about the good. I remember my mother being a beautiful, loving, spiritual and talented woman. She watched the Young and the Restless every day, she loved music and she could sew. She designed and made a lot of my clothes. She made me the most amazing Halloween costumes and some pretty funky "fashion forward" clothes. I like to believe that if she were alive today, she would have made it in the fashion world. She also loved to doll me up and experiment with my long hair. She was a housewife and a stay-at-home mom. She loved me and my little brothers. I know she did.

My father was a handsome, talented man. He worked as a shoe salesman on the Base, but his true passion was music. Before I was born, he was in a band. I remember that he played the guitar like a rock n' roll star and he could sing too. I remember getting together with family and everyone would sit around listening to my dad sing and play guitar. Sometimes my mom would sing too. They were good times and awesome memories.

Now, I will tell you about the bad...and the ugly.

My father abused drugs and my mother was an alcoholic. When it wasn't all fun and happiness, they fought...a lot. It was pretty extreme at times and when my father got angry with my mom, or with anybody for that matter, it was terrifying. He was loud and physically, verbally and mentally abusive. My parents abused each other mentally, emotionally and sometimes physically.

Over time, my mother became so severely depressed to the point that alcohol wasn't enough to take away her pain anymore. She didn't want to exist anymore and eventually, after several attempts, on November 2nd, 1981, she made that happen. The month before Christmas, 10 days after my 7th birthday and my brothers where only 3 and 5 years old. My mother was only 28! So young, so much to live for!

I know her brain was sick and she was tainted with abuse and alcohol. I know that what she did wasn't my fault, but as you can imagine, trying to figure out the meaning of life after that devastation was extremely difficult and challenging for me. It is something that I struggled with tremendously throughout most of my life.

Do I blame my father for my mother's death? I do, but only partially and he knows that. For years my father lied and told me and my brothers that my mom innocently and naturally died in her sleep. Another thing I had to struggle with until I finally found the guts to confront him and make him tell me the truth, the truth I already knew.

I don't like to talk about this era of my life in detail, but you get the gist. I will say that their abusive behavior was mainly directed towards each other and quite often, thankfully, my aunt and uncle would stay with us, play with us and take care of us.

Very soon after my mother's demise, in 1982, my father "rebounded" and re-married. I will call her the "evil stepmother". I only say that because she was truly an evil person. She would hurt me and my brothers when my father was not around and she would leave us alone as a punishment to my father when she was upset with him. After she left me and my brothers on the side of a busy highway and told us to find our own way home while she and her daughter hitchhiked back to Ottawa, my father finally saw the light and separated from her for good.

Shortly after my father's divorce from the "evil stepmother", in 1983, he met another woman who has been my stepmother ever since. She wasn't an "evil stepmother". She was actually a very nice, kind and caring person. BUT, all of this happened within a span of less than 2 years after my mom died. Imagine the pain, the confusion and the insanity. Two new "moms" and I haven't even truly had a chance to grieve or even begin to understand the loss of my real mom. I know that my father was desperate to find someone to take care of my brothers and me, but WOW it was hard. Yes, kids are resilient, but they aren't THAT resilient!

I will admit that my childhood improved significantly after my father moved in with my stepmom, despite my fears and apprehension. My new stepmom had two children and although there were conflicts at times, we all got along pretty well, like regular brothers and sisters. I do remember a lot of love, a lot of happiness and some awesome, fun times. My new stepmom wasn't my real mom, but she was the next best thing and I will refer to her as my "mom" from hereinafter.

In 1984 my father almost died from sepsis (blood poisoning) caused by a severe tooth abscess. Yes, a tooth abscess can kill you! Scary, right? Well it was very scary and I thought my dad was going to die and leave me just like my mom did. He was hospitalized in intensive care and when he didn't come home that day after my mom took him to the ER, I cried and cried. My mom tried to comfort me and assure me that he was going to be fine, but I didn't believe her and I demanded to see him so I could make sure he was still alive. My mom was told that children would not be permitted into the ICU, but she managed to convince the doctor to allow me to see him for just a few minutes. He was alive, but he was very sick and he had several tubes and machines hooked up to him. Thankfully, he pulled through and came home.

Over the next three years, my father changed his ways for the better. He had an awakening after his near-death experience. He wasn't angry all the time. He still had his moments, but for the most part, he was happy and he decided to make some positive changes. This is when I started to admire my father and truly recognize how awesome and intelligent he was. He went to college as a mature student and graduated top of his computer programming class, with distinction. As a result, he was offered an amazing job in another city. This made me really proud and that is when I truly started to realize that people really can change their negative ways and get back to good, if they put their mind to it.

In 1987, we moved from the small town of Kingston, Ontario to the big city of Ottawa, Ontario. I was 12. I was all sorts of excited and positive and optimistic. We were moving on up! Then almost immediately after we moved, my body started to change, I got my first lady flow and hit the BIG "P". Ugh! Puberty!

My Teen Years

My teen years were absolute torture. I grew into one of those super awkward teens with very low self-esteem. I had short hair, big teeth, big glasses and I looked like a boy. I also had an extreme case of acne and I was teased and bullied about it a lot. I hated the way I looked. When I would wear make-up to try and cover up the acne, people would make fun of me for wearing too much make-up. When I didn't wear make-up, they called me much worse. I couldn't win. I was often called pizza face, crater face or just plain "ugly" or "gross". One boy in junior high called me "spuds" all the time, from grade 8 to grade 10. When I finally found the guts to ask him why he was calling me that, he told me that it was because I looked like the ugly dog, "Spuds Mackenzie". Yes, that's exactly what he said. Trust me, I couldn't make that up. Random children would point at me and innocently ask their parent if I had chicken pox. That's how bad my acne was. I'm not even exaggerating one bit. It was horrible. I didn't even want to go outside of the house.

I would relentlessly pick and pick and pick at my face. I just wanted the pimples to go away and the bullying to stop. Most times, it only made the pimples worse and more noticeable. I can remember vigorously scrubbing my face and applying extra strength topical acne treatment several times a day, even at school. Eventually, I damaged and burnt the skin on my face so badly that it was raw and disgusting and I hated myself even more.

Throughout the challenges of my teen years I desperately struggled with my identity, my self-esteem and my pent up anger from my past. I let it consume me. My parents didn't understand my pain, but I never really talked about it. They were busy. They both worked outside of the house and let's face it, raising five kids wasn't easy. Eventually I just took matters into my own hands and I decided that I wasn't going to put up with the bullying at school anymore. I was just going to avoid it.

That is when I started skipping classes, which rolled into smoking, drugs, alcohol, partying and hanging out with people who were not the best of influences. When I was 15, I dropped out of high school and became an unruly and rebellious teen. The kind you hear about on the talk shows. I ran away from home several times. I put my parents though pure hell and I lived a huge LIE.

While I was living on the streets, I stayed with criminals and drug addicts. I drank heavily, sometimes to the point of blacking out and I put myself in dangerous situations all of the time. I was abused sexually, physically, emotionally and mentally, sometimes by more than one person at the same time. At one point, I was forcibly confined by a convicted sex offender that was on parole, for almost 3 days. Luckily, I escaped.

Several times, my parents came to my rescue, particularly my father. My parents were always very clear that I would always be welcome back home, as long as I followed the rules. So I would go back home, break the rules and leave again. It was a vicious cycle.

I attempted suicide a few times and I allowed a lot of people to hurt me. Sometimes I didn't allow it, but I definitely put myself in certain situations that enabled it.

I would NEVER ever accept accountability for my actions or choices. It was much easier to blame things that happened to me and people who hurt me, because I could. My birth mother killed herself and I lived a hard life, it was the perfect pity excuse for my self-destructive reckless behavior. Everyone else blames their actions on their past, it's expected right?

This teenage insanity came to a screeching halt when I found out I was pregnant at 16. This is when I finally decided that I had to make some positive changes. I needed to. My parents were not very happy about my news, but they accepted it and supported me more than I ever expected them to. Joshua was born in 1992.

Adulthood (A little sooner than it had to be)

Life as a teen mom was tough. It was definitely a rude awakening. Even though I had a lot of love and support from my family, I felt like I was whipped into another dimension! It turned out to be way different and way scarier than I imagined it would be!

My freedom was kaput and my body was ruined, physically. I expected *some* stretch marks, but not an entire stomach full of them! Holy crap! There went my bikini model days! LOL

Then, all of this happened:

In 1993 my appendix burst and I needed emergency surgery. I lived, obviously. ;)

In 1994 I was a passenger in a vehicle that was involved in a four-car "pile-up" accident that was caused by a drunk driver. I was 7 months pregnant with my second son and my oldest son, who was also in the vehicle, was 2 at the time. On impact, my belly hit the dashboard hard and I could hear the back of the car, where my son was, crunch loudly. Thankfully everyone was wearing seatbelts. I'm sure I would have gone through the windshield had I not been wearing one. When I came to and realized what happened, I frantically panicked because my baby boy wasn't making a peep in that back seat. I was so afraid to look back at his car seat, I just couldn't. His father looked back and then exclaimed, "HE'S OK! He's OK!" He was just in shock and rightfully so. Thankfully everyone in our vehicle walked away with minor injuries, but others involved in that accident were not so lucky.

In 1995 I gave birth to Jamie and I was married soon after. I truly thought that I was finally headed on a path to happily ever after. I was wrong. After less than two years of marriage, the relationship with my husband ended. He was and is still a great dad to our boys.

I sucked at marriage and at relationships in general. At times, I even sucked as a mother. Then, depression paid me a visit and all of my feelings from the past came back to haunt me. My mental health hit an all-time low, to the point that I was questioning my existence and I knew that I needed help. I didn't want to do what my mom did to me. So I made an appointment with a mental health expert.

Talking to a professional helped a lot and I did manage to keep living for my children, but I struggled, immensely.

In 1997 my step-mother developed cancer. Prior to her diagnosis, our family helplessly watched my Aunt, her sister, lose her courageous battle with breast cancer. Because of my Aunt's diagnosis, my mother was diligent about checking her own lady humps for lumps and one day, she found one. The surgery was invasive but thankfully successful. The biggest surprise was that she did not even have breast cancer. In fact, two different cancers were found. Knowing she was battling not only one, but two types of cancer was horrifying. She amazed all of us with her remarkable strength and her determination to live. Even through all of the aggressive chemo and radiation treatments, she still managed to have an awesome sense of humor and a positive outlook. She inspired me to be a better, stronger person. She was living, breathing proof of how powerful a positive attitude really was.

In 1998 I decided to go back to college as a mature student. I really wanted to make a better life for my boys. At the time, I was still a single mom. My boys and I were living with a roommate and my brother. I was working full-time nights as a domestic engineer...ok, cleaner. I was making okay money, but I wanted to be able to live on my own and not have to rely on living with others to make ends meet. So I enrolled in an accelerated full-time Administration diploma program that I attended during the day. I kept my job at night and with the help of my family, friends and my boys' father, I managed to successfully balance it all.

I graduated top of my class with "Highest Honors". It was a huge accomplishment and milestone in my life. The college I attended hired me before I completed the program. This is when I finally realized how intelligent I really was.

Life was a little easier after I went back to school. I loved being able to work a full-time administrative job during the day and I did make more money than before, but it still wasn't enough to make ends meet on my own. I really didn't consider childcare costs when I was thinking I could make it on my own. Ugh! So I decided to try bartending and waitressing part-time. It was tough to balance everything, but I managed. I loved bartending. I was good at it and I made good money, but I did miss a lot of quality time with my boys and I partied a little more than I should have. Time I will never get back.

On the evening of December 31, 1999, the New Year's Eve before Y2K,

I needed emergency surgery for an ectopic pregnancy. (I was in a relationship at the time that ended soon after this incident.) Going into an operating room at 10:30 pm when the Y2K apocalypse was scheduled to happen at midnight was a little unnerving, to say the least! Thankfully, just like all the rest of the predicted apocalypses, there was no apocalypse! ;)

In 2001, I was hit by a car. Yes. I was hit by a car, but it was totally my fault. I walked half way across the street, looked up and the light was red. For some reason, instead of just staying in the middle of the street and crossing when it was safe to do so, I panicked, didn't look both ways and ran back to the other side of the street and BAM. I got hit, but I lived...obviously. ;)

In 2002, my father learned that he had contracted Hepatitis C through blood products that he received in the 1980's. By the time he was diagnosed, it was determined that the disease had progressed to a stage that was not treatable and therefore, he was not a candidate for a liver transplant or for any treatments to prolong his life. He was terminal. When my parents informed me of this diagnosis and his prognosis, I was in a serious relationship and I was pregnant with my third child. I felt so devastated and so blessed all at the same time.

Despite the torture he endured the months following, my father was determined to meet his "first granddaughter". I didn't want to know the sex of the baby during my pregnancy, but he swore that he just knew I was having his "first granddaughter". During my pregnancy I made an extraordinary effort to spend as much time with my father as possible. At this time, my parents lived in Kingston again, so I had to travel from Ottawa to Kingston and that wasn't always easy.

As I watched the man that I loved so much wither away in front of my eyes, I learned a lot about him, a lot about the power of humor and positivity and I learned a lot about life. We both felt that it was critical for us to acknowledge and talk about the pain from the past and we did. It was cleansing. He understood that I could never forget or forgive him for the abuse that led to my mother's death and he accepted that. We had many wonderful lengthy conversations about life. We could talk and laugh for hours at a time and I made sure that he was fully aware of how proud I was of the amazing man and father he turned out to be.

Although there were a few close calls, to my amazement, my father's determination and will to live to see his "first granddaughter" paid off.

He even amazed the medical staff.

Lexie was born on March 29, 2003. My dad was too sick to visit us in the hospital, so I checked myself out early to make sure he could meet his first granddaughter ASAP. From that day, I was back and forth from Ottawa to Kingston, making sure that the kids and I spent every possible moment with my father. I knew the end was near. Then, exactly twelve days after Lexie was born and the day before his birthday, Joshua, my 10 year old son, needed emergency surgery to remove his appendix. We were all devastated and by this time, I was seriously ready to explode emotionally. I didn't know how much more I could take. But, I knew I had to stay strong for my kids and my father. So I didn't lose it. I kept on.

Thankfully Joshua healed from his surgery very quickly and we were able to share a few more quality weeks with my father. My dad asked me if I would consider moving to Kingston after he was gone so I could be close to my mom "just in case". I told him I would seriously consider it.

On May 15, 2003, my father took his final breath. Losing my father was more devastating than I could have ever imagined and as much as I thought I was prepared for it, I was in so much pain.

Life really made me angry after my father passed away. I was so fed up and I couldn't help but seriously wonder what I did to deserve all of this pain! I felt like I was being targeted and sabotaged. I felt like a trapped, scared and crazed animal. How much loss and pain should one person have to take in one lifetime?

Well, apparently the powers that BE believed that I could handle some more...

In 2004, I had emergency surgery for a second ectopic pregnancy, and then a second surgery three weeks later to remove the mess of scar tissue.

In 2005, I had emergency surgery to remove a hemorrhagic ovarian cyst that was the size of a grapefruit. I also lost my left ovary and some hormones went with it!

At this point, I let the stress of everything overwhelm me to the point that I started suffering from serious heart and blood pressure issues. It was a wakeup call. Enough was enough! I had three wonderful children to live for and I was determined to be an amazing mama, person and positive role model! So, I embarked on a mission to rid myself of all the anger and negativity.

In 2006, I decided to fulfill my father's dying wish and make the move back to Kingston. My relationship with my daughter's father was on the rocks at the time and it ended shortly after we moved. He was and still is a great father to Lexie.

It took a while to get settled into my new surroundings, but once I did, I focused on reflecting, understanding and making peace with the past. I finally acknowledged that the pain and negativity I held on to for so long, was weighing me down and I had to come to terms with it. I focused on the positives and my strengths and I took some time to learn who I really was.

I decided that I needed to forget about everything I had been taught about forgiving and forgetting, love, trust and relationships and set a new standard of reasonable expectations for myself. No more lies, no more excuses, no more depression, no more taking life way too seriously, no more false expectations and most importantly, no more setting myself up for failure. I reinvented myself and I changed my way of thinking about life, which in turn changed my way of being.

Now, I make an extra effort to find the positive, the blessings and the humor in everything, even tragic things. I can pretty much handle anything that life throws at me in a positive way. I still look back at the past, but only to remember the awesome memories, to remember the positive lessons I have learned, to help someone else learn from what I have lived and to see how far I have come.

Since my "reinvention", I have been a strong, happy, fun-loving and positive person and mama who strives to achieve awesomeness, even in the face of adversity and tragedy!

I met a wonderful, awesome "lover man" who brings out the BEST in me, accepts me and my insanity and he absolutely loves me for the person I am, even on my worst day. My children, my family and close friends also bring out the best in me and accept me for me!

Life is still tough at times. I recently had to deal with some serious health setbacks that forced me to reinvent myself AGAIN! In 2012 I had a tumor removed from the inside of my elbow and two other unrelated biopsies. The end result was painful and annoying nerve issues that I will suffer with for the rest of my life and the end of my administrative career. That is when I decided to overcome those obstacles, take advantage of some new opportunities and see if I could turn my comic strip hobby into a comic strip business.

Well, the rest is history. I now spend my days being an entrepreneur and providing a daily dose of humor and inspiration to well over 30,000 readers through the power of social media. I love doing what I do! All of this would not be possible if it wasn't for my readers and I want each and every one of you to know how much I appreciate you laughing and sharing and supporting me throughout my journey. Thank YOU!

Here's the thing...There are still moments when I do slip, trip or fall flat on my face emotionally, mentally and yes, sometimes physically (because I am very clumsy like that). I wouldn't be human if I didn't and I wouldn't be real if I didn't admit to it.

Life is hard. And sometimes, it's not just hard, it's downright INSANE! These 30 fundamental steps to awesomeness that I have established have changed my life. Now, I want to share them with you and the world.

Before we begin, I would like to make one more thing clear. I am fully aware that there are exceptions to everything and anything in life, including the steps that I have outlined in this book. Extreme circumstances or a complete loss of mental health might blow everything I have to say about achieving awesomeness right out of the water. But chances are, if you are mentally capable of reading this book and you made a choice to do so, that is not the case.

Follow me to the first step of this motivational and awesome journey.

The Steps

STEP #1

Life is HARD Expect it to BE!

©2013 Comic Strip Mama Enterprises Inc.

When I was YOUNGER, I really, REALLY wanted to be OLDER... But THIS is NOT what I EXPECTED!

©2013 Comic Strip Mama Enterprises Inc.

You got that right! When I was a little girl playing house and barbies dreaming of becoming an adult and a parent one day, THIS was not what I expected at all! When I think back to my childhood and reminisce about the times that I would think and say out loud "I can't wait to be all grown up!" I seriously wonder what the heck I was thinking. I'll tell you what I was thinking...I was sure that being all grown up would mean that I would have the freedom to do what I wanted, when I wanted, how I wanted.

Pffft. False expectation. Life is way harder and way more complicated than I ever expected it to be!

Life is like a box of chocolates?!

Ha! Even the grossest chocolate EVER is much easier to digest than some of life's blows.

I would have to say that life is more like a bag of stones! Some large...some small. You never know which one is going to be thrown at you next!

You just gotta hope for the best, expect the worst and then pick up those stones and build a firm foundation of AWESOMENESS out of them!

The HAPPIEST people are the ones who can build a FIRM foundation of AWESOMENESS out of the STONES that have been thrown at them!
AWESOME

STEP #2

Embrace the INSANITY!

©2013 Comic Strip Mama Enterprises Inc.

Are you a little bit INSANE? Yes?!

Well congratulations sunshine! YOU are perfectly and wonderfully HUMAN! Especially if you are a parent. But that will be covered in my next book. (Remember, this book is all about you as a person, not you as a parent.)

I often describe the insanity of life like a wild and crazy rollercoaster ride. Constant ups and downs, exciting and terrifying twists and turns and flipping upside down until you feel like you are hanging on to your very last shred of sanity for dear life! Yes, there are moments of calm, but they are few and far between if you are making an effort to live life to the fullest.

Yes, a healthy dose of insanity comes with the territory of living a full life. The truth is, we are all a little insane in our own special way and our mental health will be challenged on a regular basis throughout the challenges of life.

Expect it. Accept it. Own it. Have fun with it. Write a song about it! Choreograph a dance for it! Do whatever it takes to embrace it!

I used to STRUGGLE with my INSANITY, but we are friends NOW!

©2013 Comic Strip Mama Enterprises Inc.

On the other hand, an overdose of insanity is not healthy. If you sincerely feel like you cannot deal the insanity of life anymore and you feel like you are broken, speak up!

I cannot stress that enough. Mental illness is real and there IS help available. You owe it to yourself and the people who love and care for you. So please, if this is the case and you are truly struggling, read this book and then break your silence and don't wait another minute to tell someone!

STEP #3

Get Over YOURSELF!

©2013 Comic Strip Mama Enterprises Inc.

We all feel sorry for ourselves from time to time. Life is hard and it isn't always fair. Throughout the challenges of life you will be hurt by the ones you love and trust. You will experience your fair share of adversity you will also you suffer losses. Sometimes those losses will be tragic and life changing.

When you are suffering, experiencing a healthy dose of self-pity is perfectly natural and necessary. It is part of the grieving healing process. It gives you permission to let go and have a good cry. It grounds you, gives you a reality check and it SHOULD eventually make you a stronger, better person.

Excessive self-pity, on the other hand, is a powerful, destructive and overwhelming negative emotion. It affects your mental health and even your physical health. It weighs you down and holds you back. It is depressing and it can kill you. Yeah, I'm not sugar coating anything about it. Excessive self-pity can be your own worst enemy and if you wallow in it, eventually it will destroy everything in your life except for itself.

There is a very fine line between positive healthy self-pity and negative excessive self-pity and many people have a tendency to cross the line to the dark side. It's easier. It takes less effort. I know this to be true.

I felt sorry for myself excessively for a good portion my life. It was a horrible and scary existence and I experienced two major depressions as a result. Both times I was completely dysfunctional to the point that I avoided doing anything that required any amount of effort. I took a stress leave from work, I was an absent minded mother, I slept most of my life away and I shut out family and friends. I kept focusing on all of the tragedy and pain that I suffered in the past and most of the time, I didn't even care if I lived or died. I was a prisoner of my own mind. I was a victim!

Thankfully, both times I realized that I was suffering from mental illness and I needed help. As tempting as it was, leaving my children the same way my mother left me was not an option. Despite my behaviour, I knew that I wanted to be better than that.

I will be the first to admit that under certain circumstances, especially circumstances that affect you involving the death of a loved one, a tragic accident, abuse, hate crimes, natural disasters and acts of war, getting over it and getting over yourself can seem pretty impossible. But it is possible, eventually. I am living breathing proof that it IS possible! You can save yourself!

Now, ending a nasty cycle of excessive self-pity successfully is a process. I'm not going to tell you that it is as easy as telling yourself to "stop feeling sorry for yourself and you will be happy", because it's not. Also, there is nothing that anybody else can say or do to make you "snap out of it".

You need to stop negatively focusing on the "could haves" and the "should haves" and choose to focus on the positive lessons that will ultimately make you a stronger, better person going forward. You need to learn how to effectively release the anger, negativity and toxic drama. You really need to identify exactly what you are struggling with and why. That involves taking many other steps that are outlined in this book.

But there is one thought that I want you to focus on from here on in and that is this: Life is too short to be the victim. Be better, not bitter.

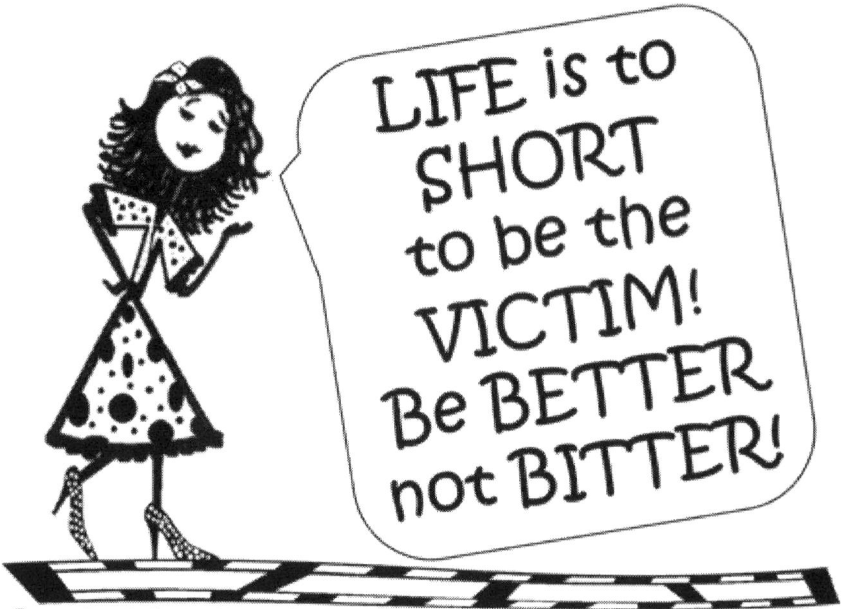
LIFE is to SHORT to be the VICTIM! Be BETTER not BITTER!

STEP #4

Give Yourself an ATTITUDE Adjustment!

Learn how to react and THINK before you SPEAK!

©2013 Comic Strip Mama Enterprises Inc.

I have often heard the saying, "My personality is ME and my attitude depends on YOU." I see this quote or variations of it plastered all over social media. It makes cringe. Especially when I see comments like "Amen!" or "You've got that right!". Hmmm. Ummmm, REALLY? I'm sorry, but it doesn't even make ANY sense!

Ahhh, yes... Now it makes perfect sense!

My PERSONALITY is ME & My ATTITUDE depends on ~~YOU~~ ME!

©2013 Comic Strip Mama Enterprises Inc.

In my opinion, anyone who believes or lives by that statement is sadly mistaken and quite frankly, a little confused. Think about it for a minute. The ONLY person that has control over YOUR attitude is YOU. I realize that there are exceptions to any rule and certain mental health factors may disable a person's ability to control their attitude and reactions. But I think for the most part, people do have control.

Your personality and your attitude go hand in hand, and together they really say a lot about the person you are. Your attitude defines your personality. Your personality refines your attitude. Together they make up your character.

> True CHARACTER is not defined by how you act when you are at your BEST! It is defined by how you react when you are at your WORST and put to the TEST!

©2013 Comic Strip Mama Enterprises Inc.

It is easy to have a bad attitude, completely LOSE IT and negatively react to negative and hurtful people or situations. It's an automatic human response to hurt, pain and fear and it requires very little thought or effort. We all experience these initial reactions. It's natural.

Having a positive attitude and reaction, on the other hand, requires a tremendous amount of effort! It's not easy to rise above the negativity and be the better person. Believe me, I know! I struggle with it too sometimes. But, if you want to be awesome, it is a necessary thing to do. I'm not suggesting that you be a coward and not say anything at all or allow people to treat you badly. No, no, no. Your response and reaction can be strong AND positive at the same time.

Here's an example...

NEGATIVE

PATHETIC

POSITIVE & AWESOME!

Hehe...

So how do you learn how to respond in a positive way? First, start thinking before you speak. Be mindful of your words and be grateful that you have the ability to say them. Look at the big picture and think about the effects that your words will have. If you are angry, think longer and harder about what you want to say before you say it!

THINK Before You Speak

- Is it **True?**
- Is it **Helpful?**
- Is it **Inspiring?**
- Is it **Necessary?**
- Is it **Kind?**

© Comic Strip Mama

Words are permanent and often hard to forget. Sometimes they can be weapons of mass destruction and really hurt and even ruin a reputation. Even your own reputation! Your mouth doesn't have an "undo" or a backspace button. Think about that. Remember that. I know sometimes I wish mine did!

Sometimes, I wish my MOUTH had "UNDO" & BACKSPACE BUTTONS!!

©2013 Comic Strip Mama Enterprises Inc.

So really think about the consequences of your responses and reactions. Think about your reputation. Think about others' reputations. Think about your integrity and always remember this:

Life is 10% what happens to you and 90% how you respond and react to it!

I wholeheartedly believe that as much as we might not want to admit it at times, we absolutely DO have control over how we react to what happens to us. Even when it really sucks.

Another thing, don't you dare be a bully!

Words have the ability to encourage, empower and heal, but they also have the ability to hurt and cause a significant amount of mental damage. Words can cut like a knife and make a person feel worthless and being a person who does this on any level is not awesome, it's awful. This is why it's SO important to THINK before you speak!

So often I hear people blame their bad attitude and behaviour on the fact that they've had a tough life. If you have had a tough life, I feel for you! I really do. But, just because your life has been tough, it doesn't mean you have to act like you are all tough and hardcore.

Just because your LIFE is TOUGH, doesn't mean you have to ACT TOUGH!

©2013 Comic Strip Mama Enterprises Inc.

Also, it's perfectly okay to say what you mean, but don't say it MEAN!

Say what you MEAN... BUT please DON'T say it MEAN!

©2013 Comic Strip Mama Enterprises Inc.

And finally, sometimes people can be downright judgemental, mean, abusive and irrational. If this is the person you are dealing with, I highly suggest you don't even waste your energy or your breath. It's not worth it. Just keep it zipped and walk away- at least until the smoke is clear!

Sometimes my GREATEST accomplishment is keeping my mouth shut and saving that energy for the ones that count!

©2013 Comic Strip Mama Enterprises Inc.

STEP #5

LEARN Who YOU Really Are!

©2013 Comic Strip Mama Enterprises Inc.

Do you really know who you are, deep down to the core?

Loaded question, right?

Well, think about it for a minute. Really think about it.

What makes you happy? What makes you angry? What makes you sad? What excites you? What terrifies you? What are you good at? What do you suck at? If you could be or do absolutely ANYTHING, what would it be and why?

What brings out the best in you? What brings out the worst?

One of the first things I had to do to "get over myself" and end my self-pity was ask myself these questions. I had to think about it all really long and hard. I had to get to know myself, my real self. Not me as a parent, just me as me. I had to identify my strengths, my weaknesses, my opportunities and my fears. Then I had to identify what brought out the best in me and what brought out the worst. I had to figure out what types of people and things I REALLY needed and wanted in my life that would make me truly happy.

Wow! What an awakening I had when I realized who I really was!

Life is so crazy and busy sometimes that we don't even think about getting to know who we really are. We just keep living and existing and doing whatever it takes to make sure everyone else is happy with what we are doing and how we are doing it. But that's not the way life should work.

Have you ever heard of a S.W.O.T. analysis? A S.W.O.T. analysis is an effective exercise that identifies your Strengths, Weaknesses, Opportunities and Threats. It is quite often used in business. I don't really like the word "Threats", I prefer "Fears" and therefore, I have changed the name to a "S.W.O.F." analysis for the purposes of this book. I think fears are easier to define than threats.

Here is an example of my own S.W.O.F analysis:

Strengths
I love myself and I BE myself.
I respect myself and others.
I'm an awesome, strong person.
I have a positive attitude and I'm optimistic.
I am a person of integrity.
I am grateful, kind and I help others.
I have an awesome sense of humor.
I love life and live it to the fullest.
I am an awesome mother.
I accept differences instead of judging.
I embrace change.

Weaknesses
I am not well spoken.
I procrastinate sometimes.
I am too paranoid sometimes.
I am too critical of myself.
I over think.
I try to do too many things at once.
I do not exercise enough.
I don't get enough sleep.
Sometimes I take on too much.

Opportunities
I learn from every experience.
I can write.
I am creative.
I can help others learn from my life.
I share and volunteer.
I have great ideas.
I am an entrepreneur.
I have amazing administrative and business skills.

Fears
Out living my children.
My children getting hurt.
Losing my physical or mental health.
FAILURE
Getting stung by a BEE. (I'm allergic)
Driving in bad weather conditions.
Public speaking.
Running out of Liquid Sanity! HA!
(Just kidding!)

Had I completed this exercise three years ago, it would have been completely different. This is an exercise that you will want to do whenever you give yourself a reality check.

In order to figure out who you truly are, it is super important to identify your strengths, weaknesses, opportunities and fears. It is absolutely essential if you want to succeed in the next steps of this book.

If you go to the resources page on my website: (www.comicstripmama.com/resources), you can print a free blank template of this S.W.O.F. analysis and complete it yourself. I encourage you to. It might seem silly, but it's important. If you are reading this book, chances are you have a little down time. So, cease this opportunity and make it a priority to learn who you really are!

Your own awesomeness starts with knowing exactly who you are!

This analysis may not reveal the person you truly aspire to be, especially if you are struggling. However, it is an important starting point so you can identify what is awesome about you and what needs to change. The

S.W.O.F. analysis is a living document that should change as you change, learn and grow.

By the time you have successfully taken all of the steps that I have outlined in this book, some of your weaknesses and fears should change to strengths and opportunities. And when they do, please send me a personal message to let me know so I can congratulate you personally! ;)

STEP #6

Discover Your Purpose!

BE Yourself!
RESPECT Yourself!
LOVE Yourself!

©2013 Comic Strip Mama Enterprises Inc.

Are you desperately struggling to figure out your purpose in life? Well, if you are, you are not alone! I spent a good chunk of my life doing exactly that until one day I discovered that I was totally complicating it with over thinking. Then, I had a EUREKA! moment and finally figured it out!
Ultimately, your purpose in life is to survive, BE the BEST person you can be while you are on the face of this earth and contribute to the world in a positive way. Remember that I am concluding that your goal in life is to be the best awesome person you can be, since you making an effort to read this book!

BE YOURSELF, RESPECT yourself & LOVE yourself so the RIGHT people will LOVE and RESPECT the REAL YOU!

©2013 Comic Strip Mama Enterprises Inc.

How do you achieve this? Again, another simple answer that we often complicate with over thinking. All you have to do is be yourself, respect yourself and love yourself. When you practice these three things, you will be a strong, positive and happy person. When you are a strong, happy and positive person, you become a magnet for all of these things and the powerful energy that you exude will be contagious! When you realize all of this and practice it, then you will realize your true self-worth!

I say it's a simple answer, yet "being yourself" is such a hard thing to do in this life! It seems to be much easier to be something you are not, but it's probably the most self-destructive thing you can do. We tend to believe that it is necessary to do so in order to please people or to achieve certain things. More often than not, we end up realizing that these people and things are not genuinely what we need in our life because they were acquired for the wrong reasons.

Think about a person you know that acts completely different around different people. We often refer to these people as being "fake" or "two-faced". Perhaps you are or have been one of these people. If you are one, I hope that you are reading this book in an effort to change that about yourself.

I was a fake person for many years, but I eventually learned that being a fake person is very transparent and you end up surrounding yourself with the wrong people and things for the wrong reasons. You also completely confuse the people who genuinely love and care for you and you end up pushing them out of your life because they feel like they can't trust you. And they shouldn't. Fake people lie, deceive, use people and talk about people negatively when they aren't around to defend themselves. Sound familiar? It's okay. You can change this about yourself.

Do not to allow other people, things and situations define who YOU ARE. Especially negative ones. It's ok to learn from and allow other people, things and situations *help* you recognize who you truly are or are not, but there is a huge difference between recognizing and defining. You need to define yourself on your own terms. Identifying your strengths, your weaknesses, your opportunities and fears will help you do this. If you are still having trouble analyzing them, ask a close friend or family member to *help* you. Then try again. Remember that this analysis might not reveal the person you truly aspire to be, especially if you are struggling at present. However, it is an important starting point so you can identify what is awesome about you and what needs to change.

Perhaps it would help to think about it this way: If you were to die today, what would you want your eulogy to say about you?

Really think about how you want people to remember you and then work towards being that person.

I once had a BFF tell me that I was like a "ray of sunshine" and that I could light up a room simply because I was present. She said that no matter how down she was feeling I could always make her laugh and feel better about life because I encouraged her to find the positive, the blessings and the humor in everything, even tragic things. When I was around her, I was my TRUE self. It was easy. She was one of my best friends so I felt safe letting my guard down around her and just doing and being and saying exactly what came natural to me in any given situation. Most of the time, I just laughed about the insanity of life, but it was okay because she laughed too. I focused on that. Then, I embarked on a mission to BE that person in every aspect of my life.

> I'm NOT AWESOME like YOU... I'M AWESOME like ME!

©2013 Comic Strip Mama Enterprises Inc.

Being YOU is the most important thing you can be in this life. Loving yourself and respecting yourself is what comes next.

Love and respect yourself enough to BE who you really are and not what other people want you to be. BE and DO what makes you happy and you will be awesome!

Now, I have often heard the saying, "Sometimes telling someone to be themselves and do what makes them happy is the worst advice ever." I feel the need to acknowledge this. If being miserable and negative and angry and hurting others makes you happy, don't be yourself. You desperately need to change. But, chances are if you are reading this book, you probably don't live an evil existence. I hope.

Also, if being yourself means that you do stand out and you are a little different from what other people in your life perceive to be the "norm", then for the love of everything holy, BE a proud, happy, strong, positive person and OWN IT. Don't play mister or miss victim when people point your differences out or even judge you for them. There is no such thing as "normal". We are all different.

Remember, life is too short to play the victim! Yes, I agree that in a perfect world, people would just accept and respect differences, but this isn't a perfect world. It can be a very cruel and ignorant world sometimes. You can't change every cruel and ignorant person in the world, but you can change how YOU react to them. Don't react negatively to cruel or ignorant people and turn into an angry, hateful person. It's better to react in a positive, but strong way. Remember you can still stand up for yourself and be positive about it. I know it's hard, but you can do it. It just takes a little more effort.

I am judged negatively for a lot of the things that I have done in life and even for the person I am today. I am judged because I was a teenage mom. I am judged because my sons have a different father than my daughter. I am judged because I struggled with relationships. I am judged because I drink alcohol and I am a mom. I am judged because I still like to celebrate and party sometimes. I am judged because I take time for myself. I am judged because I don't take life as seriously as others. I am judged because I accept differences. I am judged because of my spiritual beliefs. I could go on and on and on and on.

But the way I see it is people can judge me all they want. Any mistakes that I have made, I have learned positive lessons from and made positive changes as a result. My only intention in life is simply to be an awesome person and to live in harmony with others. I love myself and I respect myself enough to I stand behind who I truly am regardless of what others think, say and feel about it. Like me, love me and accept me for who I am, or leave me alone. Having said that, I am also respectful person so I don't go around with a "like it or suck it" attitude and neither should you.

If my intentions in life were not good ones and I was still on a reckless path of self-destruction or if I was intentionally hurting and inflicting physical or mental pain upon others, then I would deserve to be judged. But this is not the case. I know that I'm an awesome person and mother despite what other closed minded people might think and that is all that matters.

I love and accept other awesome people for who they REALLY are too. I don't care what you look like, what you do for a living, how rich you are, how poor you are, who you love or what you believe in just as long as you are making the best effort to be a good person and your intentions are not hurtful or evil. If you are truly an honest to goodness person, I accept you for who you are regardless of whether or not I would choose to look like you, believe like you or live your lifestyle. Period.

I encourage you with every fibre of my being to open your mind and do the same. <3

STEP #7

Make Peace With Your Past!

> FORGET everything you have been told about FORGIVING FORGETTING & TRUST!

©2013 Comic Strip Mama Enterprises Inc.

Yes, you read that correctly. I am encouraging you to forget about everything you have been told about forgiving, forgetting and trust! If you do this, I promise that you will look at everything in life differently, in a positive way!

This step made the most difference in my life and every chance I get I encourage others to follow it. It is amazing how much my life changed instantly for the better once I made this discovery.

First, let's focus on forgiving and forgetting. We are conditioned to believe that we should always forgive and forget in order to be truly happy in life. It is drilled into our heads. Doctors, therapists and self-help experts tend to focus on it being the *key* to letting go of the past and living a wonderful, happy and fulfilling life! Well, I think the whole cliché, "forgive and forget" should be abolished! Most times, asking someone to forgive and forget is asking the impossible of a person. What happens is they just end up struggling and lying to themselves instead of truly healing. This ultimately results in failure.

Forgiving someone *might* be possible, but don't count on it. The truth is, most things that we struggle to forgive are unforgivable and that is why we struggle. **Forgetting** anything, especially tragic and painful things, is pretty much impossible. Unless of course you have amnesia, in which case you would be struggling to remember instead of struggling to forget. You can't just erase your memory. It's not built that way. Yet so many people die trying, because they are *told* they should.

Now let's focus on **trust**. Many people assume that important relationships between parents, children, life partners, other blood relatives and best friends should automatically establish a level of trust. While trust is a necessary foundation of any important relationship, it still must be earned and built over time. Even once it is established, I wholeheartedly believe that it is not reasonable or wise to trust ANY person, including yourself, a 100%!

Humans are born to make mistakes, we are not perfect. If you think about it, more often or not, the ones we love the most disappoint, betray and hurt us the most, because they matter the most.

I trust the people I love and care for the most about 90%. This is something that I am very open and honest about and I expect the same level of trust in return. I think this is a reasonable and wise expectation.

Remember, we are only human. We all make mistakes. Sometimes our minds change, our feelings change and outside influences can have an impact on even our best of intentions! If you think you can trust anyone fully and completely, you are fooling yourself and setting yourself up for major disappointment and failure. Have realistic expectations!

Now let me tell you how I figured all of this stuff out for myself:

When I sought therapy for my first depression, shortly after my separation from my ex-husband, I poured my heart out to my therapist. She was truly a wonderful, compassionate person and it felt so good to break my silence and let it all out. It was obvious that most of my pain and self-torment was a result of me being so angry with my birth mother for taking her own life and never really coming to terms with it. I truly blamed my mother for most of the pain, abuse and anger that happened in my life. I believed that if she didn't do what she did, my life would have been different. It would have somehow been better.

At the end of my first therapy session, my therapist told me to go home that night and write a letter to my mom. She told me not to hold anything back and write the letter as if I had an opportunity to be face to face with her one last time. So that is exactly what I did. The letter was several pages long and it was FULL of overwhelming emotion. My subsequent therapy sessions focused on different parts of that letter. After every session, I felt a new sense of relief. I felt like I was getting back to good.

On my final day of therapy, my therapist took my letter out of my hands and said. "When you leave here today, I want you to forgive your mother, forgive your father and every person that ever hurt you. I want you to forget all of the pain from the past and learn to trust and love again." Then she asked me if I thought I could do it. I enthusiastically responded "Yes! I can do it now!". I thanked her, gave her a big hug and walked out of that office with determination, the best of intentions and my head held high. I truly thought I was over it ALL and at peace with my past.

Then I struggled...and I struggled...and I struggled some more as life hit me with some more blows. As much as I kept telling myself that I could forgive, I could forget and I could trust fully again, I just couldn't do any of it.

Right before my father passed away, we had a conversation. He finally opened up to me about the past. We talked about a lot of things in great detail. We discussed life before and after my mother's demise and I told my father that I couldn't forgive my mother or forgive him for hurting her and not helping her. Then he said, "It's okay, you don't have to and you shouldn't. We don't deserve your forgiveness." At that moment, I felt as if a huge weight lifted off of my chest.

Then I hit another depression just before I decided to make my move to Kingston and I struggled, and struggled and struggled some more. I couldn't afford therapy at the time, but I knew I needed help. At first, I shut down and shut people out of my life, just like I did before. But, then I realized that these people that loved and cared about me really wanted to help me. And so I decided to break my silence. I reached out to them and I talked and talked and talked about everything that I was struggling with. THAT is when I finally had the revelation!

I finally realized that the reason I was struggling SO much for SO many years was simply because I was expecting the impossible from myself. No matter how much I *told* myself that I *needed* to forgive and forget and trust again, it wasn't happening because it was a completely unreasonable expectation! THIS is what I had to come to terms with. Once I discovered that, I figured out what I really needed to do to heal and make peace with the past, once and for all.

I didn't *need* to struggle anymore.

I didn't *need* to expect the impossible of myself.

I didn't *need* to forgive.

I didn't *need* to forget.

I didn't *need* to trust anyone fully.

All I really needed to do to truly make peace with the past was this:

> **ACCEPT** *the things you cannot change;*
> **LEARN** *positive lessons;*
> **RECOGNIZE** *the blessings;*
> **REMEMBER** *the awesome times;*
> **FIND** *the humor whenever possible; and*
> **TRUST REASONABLY**, *but never fully,*
> *so you can keep on keepin' on, hoping for the best and being prepared for the worst!*

©2013 Comic Strip Mama Enterprises Inc.

Accept the things you cannot change. Learn positive lessons, recognize the blessings, remember the awesome times and find the humor whenever possible. And trust reasonably. Don't expect that the ones you love the most will *never* hurt you or betray you. Trust is earned, and remember this goes both ways.

If you find yourself consistently having "trust issues" and suspecting that a person is betraying you, taking you for granted, cheating on you or worse, you must confront that person, talk about it and figure things out. If you are having the trust issues because you made a choice to continue a relationship with someone who has hurt you or betrayed you, perhaps you should seriously ask yourself if it's healthy and worth it to remain in the relationship.

I promise you, all of these things are achievable and reasonable expectations of ANY person in ANY circumstance. Even tragic circumstances! I encourage you to live by them.

STEP #8

Accept Accountability!

©2013 Comic Strip Mama Enterprises Inc.

> I don't know about YOU, but I have thought about RUNNING AWAY way more as an ADULT than I EVER did as a KID!

©2013 Comic Strip Mama Enterprises Inc.

It's TRUE! And I was a "RUNAWAY"!

Do you ever feel like you would much rather run away and hide from your problems, your mistakes and your failures rather than face them and own up to them?

Yeah, me too. And shamefully, I did this for many years.

Not only did I run away from my problems, I took it a step further and blamed others and my tragic childhood for my negative attitude, my poor choices and my reckless, self-destructive behavior.

I mean, given my tragic past, it was perfectly normal and excusable to do so...Right? Even my therapist said so.

Well, if you agreed with that, I'm disappointed, but not surprised.

We live in a world that rationalizes and justifies sometimes immoral, evil behavior every single day without holding the actual individual accountable. It's insane how much this happens. For example, when I was a teen and I was arrested and charged with being an accomplice to a break and enter. I didn't enter the home, but I "kept six" as they called it. My lawyer questioned me and asked me why I did it, why I was living on the street, why I was being a rebellious teen hanging out with criminals, etc...So I pulled the victim card. I told him that I had a hard life and my mom committed suicide when I was seven and BAM! That's all I needed to say. That is what he used to plead my case and I got off with a slap on the hand! This kinda stuff happens all the time.

Now let's be realistic, I wasn't a rebellious runaway teen living on the streets hanging out with criminals and making my parents life a living hell because I had a hard life OR because my mom committed suicide. I had a good life waiting for me at home and yes, I was having a hard time dealing with my tragic childhood, but it was really no excuse. I did all of those things because I chose to and I knew I could blame my negative attitude, my bad choices and my reckless self-destructive behavior on my past. THAT's the real reason.

I know that a lot of times, we are not responsible for certain tragic circumstances that occur throughout the challenges of life. Sometimes things happen that are beyond our control such as the death of a loved one, tragic accidents, abuse, natural disasters and acts of war. However, I do believe that we eventually have control of your own final outcome, providing you are old enough to know better. In other words, if your world is turned upside down, how you react and respond is your choice. Unless your mental state *legitimately* makes it impossible.

Like I always say, there are blessings and positive lessons to be found in everything, even tragic things. If you insist on wallowing in self-pity and reacting negatively, you need to accept accountability for your actions, words and behavior as a result.

We are all human. We all bend and break rules. We all lose it and react negatively at times. We all do things we are not proud of. We all hurt other people and make mistakes. Just own up to it! Trust me, you will feel so much better about yourself and about life!

Do you want to know what really terrifies me? If I didn't have people in my life that genuinely loved and cared about me as much as they did, I don't know that I would have been able to find the strength to accept accountability and make the necessary positive changes to become the person that I am today. Even a mental health professional and a lawyer sent me back out into the world to fail because they made me believe that my behaviour was normal and excusable. How many people do you think have nobody to love and care for them enough to help them get through mental struggles? There are lots of them and that is scary.

I lose my breath when I think about the fact that I could have continued on my path of reckless self-destruction and turned out to be a low-life, abusive, drug-addicted alcoholic mother with absolutely no ambition to do anything good with my life and that would have been perfectly acceptable to many people, because of my tragic past. Think about that.

We all need to make a better effort to help those that have no one in their life that genuinely gives a crap about them. I don't care if they tell you they love living on the streets or they don't want to change. Do you really expect that a person like that is going to trust anything that anyone has to say to them at first?

Probably not. They need to be shown how awesome life really can be! This is primarily why I am writing this book.

I realize this is easier said than done, but the effort to do something about it can be made slowly but surely. =)

"We are NOT afraid that the WORLD will end... We are AFRAID that the WORLD will continue without CHANGING ANYTHING!"

©2013 Comic Strip Mama Enterprises Inc.

STEP #9

Stop Setting Yourself Up for FAILURE!

LOWER your expectations of yourself!

©2013 Comic Strip Mama Enterprises Inc.

Are you trying to be a little too AWESOME?

As much as I hate to admit it...Yes, there is such a thing!

And this is what usually happens as a result:

> Sometimes... I SMILE just to hide how COMPLETELY OVERWHELMED I AM!

©2013 Comic Strip Mama Enterprises Inc.

Yes, we keep smiling and trying to do and be everything to everyone, but all we are REALLY doing is setting ourselves up for failure!

Despite being completely overwhelmed and exhausted, we continue to bite way more than we can possible chew which usually leaves us feeling overworked and undervalued, underappreciated and sometimes, underpaid.

And then one day...

We are "Awesome Exhausted"!

This is what I mean by "Awesome Exhausted"!

Doesn't matter how awesome you are, we ALL have our LIMITS!

Now that I have decided to be an entrepreneur on top of being a person with a life to live, a mama with 3 children to raise and a wifey to a lover man who has needs, I have really had to think about my limits a lot. Even if you do not wear the exact same hats that I do, you most likely still face some of the exact same challenges and insanity that I face on a daily basis.

The truth is, sometimes we are our own worst enemy when it comes to setting ourselves up for failure. We procrastinate, we aren't organized, we try to do too many things at once and we try to be everything to everyone *all the time.*

Allow me to humor you and make light of the ways that I get "awesome exhausted" and end up failing as a result. Perhaps you can relate! ;)

"ADID" — Attention Deficit IDEA Disorder, otherwise known "Ideaitis", is primarily caused by having WAY too many awesome ideas and too little time and brain power to possibly effectively and efficiently execute all of them at the same time!

Solution:

Keep a record of all of the ideas and then work on one, maybe two at a time. Refer back to the wish list of ideas and repeat.

"I suffer from ADOD. Attention Deficit Organization Disorder! It's where you start organizing one thing, but get distracted by other things and then the kids need something, then the phone rings, then you have to find something and then you make a mess of everything you just organized only to end up being LESS organized than you were when you started!"

"ADOD" — Attention Deficit Organization Disorder, otherwise known as "Organizationitis", is commonly caused by not making a conscious effort to put things back where they belong, even when you have a system set up to aide you with your efforts.

Solution:

Keep things organized and take the extra seconds or minutes to just put things back where they belong.

"ADCD" — Attention Deficit Cleaning Disorder can cause extreme confusion and exhaustion because you know that you feel extremely exhausted, but you just can't see why because everything is half-done!

Solution:

Try to only focus and clean one thing or at least stick to one room at a time. This might require that you lock yourself in a room until you have finished cleaning it!

"PD" — Procrastination Disorder is commonly caused by...I'll finish this later.....

Solution:

"SD" — Sleeping Disorder is primarily caused by the little nocturnal voice in your head that wants to stay up, have a little chitty chat and repeatedly go over your invisible to do list in your head!

Important notice: "SD"- Sleeping Disorder is also quite commonly caused by an internet connection and a device that connects to it!

Solution:

Ignore that voice in your head and stop taking mobile devices to bed with you.

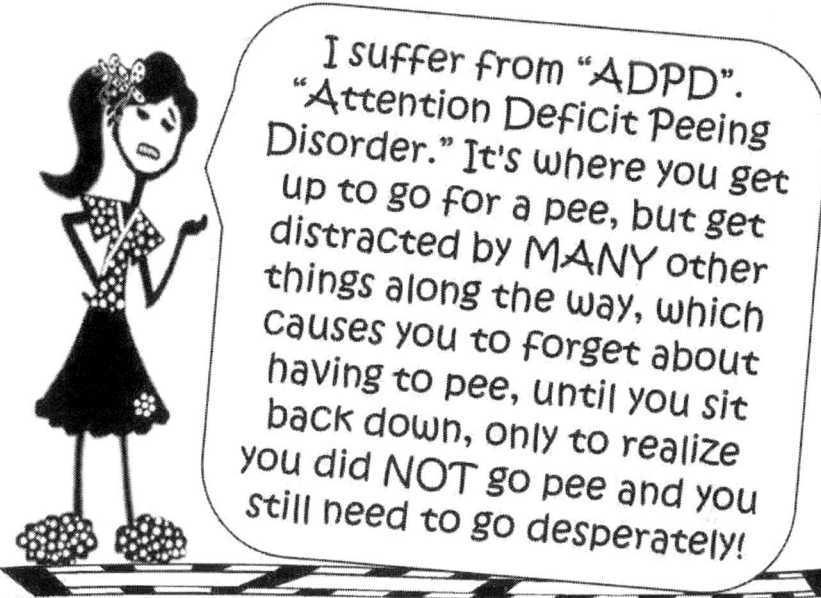

> I suffer from "ADPD". "Attention Deficit Peeing Disorder." It's where you get up to go for a pee, but get distracted by MANY other things along the way, which causes you to forget about having to pee, until you sit back down, only to realize you did NOT go pee and you still need to go desperately!

©2013 Comic Strip Mama Enterprises Inc.

"ADPD" — Attention Deficit Peeing Disorder commonly occurs when you suffer from all of the other disorders that are outlined in this book!

Solution:

Google "holding your pee" and take a look-see. When you learn about the health risks and that holding your pee can cause your bladder to strrreeeetttchh and turn into a breeding ground for infection, um, well...you might think about those things instead of all the distractions along the way to the washroom the next time you need to go. But, let's be honest, sometimes distraction will still win!

I must admit, I am a work in progress when it comes to learning how NOT to do these things. They seem to be my nemesis! The things I love to hate about my brain and how it functions.

If you can relate to any of these, let's work together to change! You gotta realize that there is only so much that you can expect from yourself and sometimes our brains just need a break.

So don't spread yourself too thin and ask for help if you need to. Say yes when you can, but say no when you can't. If you don't know if you can or can't, say "Let me get back to you!"

STEP #10

Try Not to Assume!

> Form your OWN opinions!

©2013 Comic Strip Mama Enterprises Inc.

We all make assumptions instead of asking questions sometimes. I try really hard not to make assumptions. But, I'm not going to lie and tell you that I don't, because I definitely do from time to time.

I assume mostly because I'm *afraid* of asking questions or perhaps I misunderstand or misinterpret something that someone has said or done. I'm not going to tell you that you should *never* assume anything because in all honesty, it's not a reasonable expectation and I don't expect the impossible from anyone anymore. There are just too many factors in today's world that cause people to assume.

What I will tell you is never pass up an opportunity to ask questions when possible and always ask for clarification of words or actions, or lack thereof, if necessary. Especially when you are taken aback by a text message or an email or a comment on a social media platform. All too often we misinterpret the intent of these messages.

I am going to encourage you to never base your opinion of someone or something solely based on another person's opinion. Even if they are a close friend or family member. This is a terrible thing to do and I can honestly tell you that I do not do this. I refuse. As long as I am blessed with the ability to form my *own* opinion, I will do just that.

It's not that I don't value what other people say. I quite often consider other people's opinions and I love learning from others too. However, my final opinion of someone or something is based on what I have seen with my own eyes, what I have heard with my own ears and what I have felt with my own heart. Period.

I learned how important it is to form your OWN opinion the hard way.

A few times in this life I have missed out on precious time with certain people because of what I *heard* about them and then later in life found out that they were really awesome and amazing! I have also missed out on opportunities.

So, take it from me! It's worth it to make the effort to see, hear and feel for yourself.

And this is my lil' comic take on this entire step:

Never ASSUME that I share YOUR OPINION!

©2013 Comic Strip Mama Enterprises Inc.

STEP #11

Release Anger, Negativity & Toxic Drama!

©2013 Comic Strip Mama Enterprises Inc.

We all suffer from anger and negativity throughout the challenges of life and a lot of times it results in directly or indirectly causing some kind of toxic drama. I say "suffer" because being angry and negative IS truly painful. It inflicts pain on yourself and it inflicts pain on others. The stress of it all can even affect your mental and physical health.

Nevertheless, anger and negativity are part of our complex set of human emotional responses. We all have a right to be angry and disappointed sometimes. I never suggest that you hold anger in to fester. In order to truly live a happy and awesome in life, it is healthy and necessary to acknowledge it, deal with it, express it and then release it, but in a positive way. This is the way I see it:

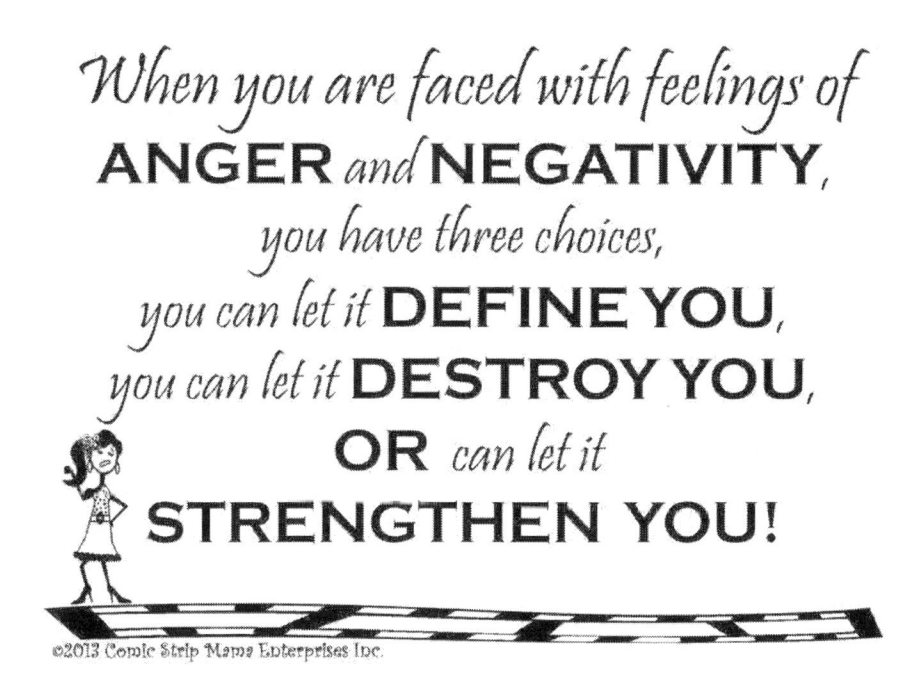

When you are faced with feelings of **ANGER** *and* **NEGATIVITY**, *you have three choices*, *you can let it* **DEFINE YOU**, *you can let it* **DESTROY YOU**, **OR** *can let it* **STRENGTHEN YOU!**

©2013 Comic Strip Mama Enterprises Inc.

If you let anger and negativity DEFINE you, you will become an angry and negative person. You will intentionally look for the negative in everything and everyone and wallow in your negativity. People will avoid you for fear that you will just bring them down. THAT is a miserable existence and eventually, if you don't do something about it, it will destroy you.

If you let anger and negativity DESTROY you, you will lose complete control of your emotions and reactions. You will abuse people and things with your words and your power. You will become a serious danger to yourself and everyone around you. People won't *really* listen to your concerns, your fears or your beliefs. All they will hear is your anger. You might think that your anger is effective, because you *think* that people are listening to you and taking you seriously, but in reality they are just scared. People will want to run far, far away from you, and rightfully so. You may also find yourself having to answer to the law for your behavior and your actions.

If you let anger and negativity STRENGTHEN you, you will acknowledge it, deal with it, express it and release it in a positive way. You will motivate people to listen to your concerns, your fears and your beliefs. You will prevent others from walking away from you, walking all over you and you will be respected for it. You will think about consequences and avoid hurting others.

When acknowledging your anger and negativity, you need to ask yourself why you're feeling those emotions and then figure out how you are going to deal with it. If you have already had a little verbal or physical outburst, then take a minute to breathe and think. Most times our outbursts are not necessary and they are often hurtful, so if that is the case and you have negatively affected another person with your actions or words, apologize.

When expressing your anger, it's fine to say what you mean, but don't say it mean. And, try really hard not to use the words "you never" and "you always". They suck. Telling a person that they "never" or "always" do something is, #1) a lie and #2) a huge overreaction. It's pretty much impossible for someone to "always" or "never" do something. But it's easy for us to only focus on a person doing or not doing the thing that we are upset about when we are angry. My youngest son handed these words to me on a platter one day when I basically told him that he "never" helped out around the house without being asked and he "always" had to be told to do everything! Of course this is not true. Sometimes they do need to be asked and reminded, but all of my kids make an effort to help out around the house without being asked. My son's response was, "Well, I guess I shouldn't do anything anymore without being asked because you obviously don't care or appreciate the stuff that I do anyway." Yeah, that's what happens when you don't think before you speak. Not only were my words completely untrue, they were hurtful and degrading.

When releasing your anger, the key is simply communicating in a calm positive way. If I'm too emotional, in most cases, I will tell the person(s) directly involved in the situation that I need space and time to think before I communicate. If I think that a conversation might result in more negative anger and confrontation, I will communicate how I'm feeling in some other way.

I used to write letters, but now I send emails or text messages. ;) Yes, I agree that a face to face conversation is always better, but not if you avoid communicating altogether because you can't. If communicating by other means other than talking face to face is the only way you are going to get things off your chest, do it. I don't care what anybody says, it is way better than holding it all in!

And finally, when releasing your anger, cry if you need to and try really hard to find the blessings, the positive lessons and the humor in the situation!

> Have a good CRY if you need to and a good LAUGH if you can!

©2013 Comic Strip Mama Enterprises Inc.

Now, there's always another side to every coin. Not only do we have to deal with our own anger and negativity throughout the challenges of life, we must deal with others' anger and negativity as well.

I always try to see the good in everything and everyone. I always try to give a person the benefit of the doubt. I always try to make people laugh and use humor to lighten people up. I always try to encourage people to focus on the blessings and the positive lessons in everything. I always try to challenge negative thinking and turn it into positive thinking. BUT sometimes despite my best efforts, there is no convincing some people to stop being angry and negative!

The truth is...

> ANGER, NEGATIVITY & DRAMA! Some people just LOVE to SPRINKLE that stuff on EVERYTHING!

©2013 Comic Strip Mama Enterprises Inc.

They seem to thrive on it!

My formula for dealing with people I encounter in life who insist on being angry and negative and cause toxic drama is this:

- Acknowledge that they are feeling angry and negative.
- Try to get them to focus on the good, the positive, the blessings and attempt to help them deal with and express their emotions in a positive way.
- Give them a hug and try to make them laugh and stop taking life way too seriously.
- Try to convince them to let the anger and negativity strengthen them instead of defining or destroying them.
- Try to get them to eliminate the "could have", "should have" thinking and focus on the positive lessons that were learned as a result.

If an angry and negative person refuses to respond to any of my best efforts, then I simply tell them that I'm all out of strength, energy and time. I might also suggest that they seek help that I obviously cannot provide. Then I make sure they know that they are very welcome to come back into my life when they decide they want to be a happier, better person. Period.

Life is too short to allow yourself to be poisoned with anger, negativity and toxic drama when a person simply refuses to get past it and insists on wallowing in it. So don't do it. Just like you must release your own anger and negativity, you must release angry and negative people who cause you drama and grief when they have nothing else to offer you.

Sometimes you just have to come to terms with this. It doesn't make you a bad person. It makes you a smart person because you realize that it is necessary and in your best interest.

Depending on where you are running into all of the negativity and anger and toxic drama in your life, you may not be able to *completely* avoid it. If it's happening at work or at school or during family or social engagements, you might have to make the choice to be the bigger person, keep your lips sealed and just tolerate it. I always encourage speaking up and removing negativity, anger and toxic drama from your life, however, sometimes it's just not that easy. In these situations, you just must avoid it as much as possible and choose to be happy!

> I am by NO means oblivious to all of the anger, negativity and toxic drama going on around me... I just CHOOSE to AVOID it and be HAPPY and AWESOME!

©2013 Comic Strip Mama Enterprises Inc.

And always remember this...

> People will tell you, "You don't know what you've got until it's gone"... But sometimes you know exactly what you HAD and that's why your life is better, because it's GONE!

©2013 Comic Strip Mama Enterprises Inc.

On a lighter, humorous note, sometimes the only way you can avoid negativity, anger and toxic drama is to do what I do and imagine yourself in an "awesome bubble"! Sounds a little crazy, but HEY, it works for me! ;)

STEP #12

Get Over Your False Sense of ENTITLEMENT!

FEEL GRATEFUL, NOT ENTITLED!

©2013 Comic Strip Mama Enterprises Inc.

I want you to think about everything in your life at this very moment.

Think about your physical and mental health, your human rights, the people you love, the job you have, the business you run (if applicable), the people that work for you including caregivers, housekeepers, employees, etc. (if applicable), the vehicle you drive, the place you live, the clothes you own, the "toys" you have, the food you are able to eat and luxuries you are able to afford.

©2013 Comic Strip Mama Enterprises Inc.

Now answer this question honestly:

Are you truly grateful for everything in your life at this moment OR do you feel like you are "entitled" to it?

What would you do if all of it, or even *some* of it, was taken away tomorrow? Then what?

I know that it is a terrible thing to think about, but it happens to people every single day. In a heartbeat, one "disaster" could potentially take it all or some of it away in one fell swoop!

If you live your life thinking you're entitled to certain people, certain things and a certain standard of living, you seriously should think about what you would do if you didn't have it all tomorrow? What would your reaction be? Would you snap and do whatever it took to get everything back, even something not moral? Or, do you think you would wallow in self-pity and live the rest of your life miserably? OR, would you be grateful for what is left, accept the fact that you need to start over again, reinvent yourself and move on?

I know we all would like to believe that we are entitled to certain people, certain things and a certain standard of living. Many of us work extremely hard to achieve the things we have in this life. I have also had to work hard for everything in my life. However, I have made a conscious effort to stop thinking I'm entitled to anything and start feeling grateful for everything.

I have lived and lost enough in this life to truly understand that this life doesn't owe me or you a thing. Nothing.

We are all born and we will all die. These are the two *real* certainties of life for any living, breathing creature on this earth, including humans. Everything else is circumstantial and not guaranteed. It's all *stuff* that you should be grateful for because it's all *stuff* that you can lose in a split second.

Think about it. You can *lose* your physical and mental health. You can *lose* your human rights. You can *lose* the people you love. You can *lose* your job. You can *lose* your business. You can *lose* the people that work for you. You can *lose* your vehicle. You can *lose* the place you live. You can *lose* your clothes, food, "toys" and luxuries you are able to afford.

I think you should always feel grateful and never feel entitled, regardless of how much you believe you have earned something. The world is such a huge mess because of people feeling less grateful and more entitled.

We complain that "kids today" are the "entitled generation", but take a good look at the world. Are you really surprised? I'm not. Entitlement fosters greed. The more we have, the more we want and often, we don't take time to be just grateful! It's so important.

Think about something you absolutely believe you are entitled to.

Now finish this sentence:

I am **entitled** to_____
because_____

Now replace the word "entitled" with "grateful" and replace whatever comes after "because" with "I am blessed and fortunate".

Yes, you may have worked your bootie off to earn and achieve everything in your life and get to where you are today, but you should still feel grateful, not entitled. You should also recognize all of the people, things, experience, life lessons, circumstances and your physical and mental ability that has made it all possible.

So instead of feeling entitled, and attaching all your happiness to *stuff* that circumstances might change tomorrow, look at life through grateful eyes and feel blessed and fortunate for what you have today. <3

STEP #13

Live SIMPLY Within Your Means!

©2013 Comic Strip Mama Enterprises Inc.

I am a simple modest person materialistically. It does not take a lot to make me happy and I don't measure a person's worth or how much they care for me by how much money they are willing to spend on me. Ever.

Diamond rings, designer labels, the finest, the most expensive things and all of those fancy material things really don't impress me much. I just cannot justify the sometimes crazy outrageous costs when I'm perfectly comfortable with spending less.

That's just me. If those kinda things impress you and are important to you, that is your choice. But maintaining that high lifestyle can make life a little more complicated and disappointing than it has to be.

I know what it is like to struggle to keep a roof over my head, feed myself and my children and pay for the bare necessities of life. I know what it is like to live paycheck to paycheck. I know what it's like to lose everything and have to start over again. I don't like having a lot to lose and I don't like having a lot of "frivolous things" when other people are struggling just to have the essential and necessary things.

I do work very hard to earn a living, so I do like to be able to reward myself and have nice things, but I am very practical about everything I spend money on. I dress nicely and fashionably, but I ain't too proud to admit that most of my wardrobe and accessories were purchased from discount stores, thrift stores and clearance racks! I also enjoy convenience, but only if I can justify the price.

I do like to live a comfortable life, but being able to give generously when I can is also very important to me. If I ever made the "big time", I would buy a nice home, travel with my special ones and give very generously to my family, friends and charities. I would also give to random people in need. This is my dream.

I believe that money cannot buy *true* happiness, but I also realize that we unfortunately cannot really live without it. The ideal life is to have both, but not if you are sacrificing one for the other or watching other people suffer as a result. Some people are living happy, fulfilling lives with much less than you have! Remember that!

I believe that it is super important for people to live within their financial means as much as possible. Making good property, education, business and retirement investments is one thing, but going into major consumer debt to maintain a certain standard of living is a killer. So many people are drowning in consumer debt and this type of financial crisis is a heavy burden that destroys people and families. I know! Consumer debt haunted me for many years and it took a very long time to repair it. I'm kind of grateful that it happened to me when I was younger because the experience taught me some very valuable lessons that I will never forget. The most valuable lesson was that I could live simply, within my means and still have an awesome, happy life!

I might not have the finest things in life, but I am blessed because I am happy and I truly value everything, especially all of the people in my life. That is what *truly* matters.

STEP #14

Don't Succumb to Your Weaknesses & Fears!

©2013 Comic Strip Mama Enterprises Inc.

Heheh...Ummm NO it doesn't!

You should never run away from your weaknesses and fears no matter how hard they are to face. You just need to change your way of thinking about them.

It is healthy and human for you to have *some* weaknesses and fears. They keep you "down to earth" and they are part of the genuine person you are. Quite often we see our weaknesses and fears as negative attributes, but you shouldn't.

Above all else, I fear anything that might threaten the lives of my children. However, my children have taught me that you can't deprive yourself of living life and doing the things that you love simply because there is a *chance* that the worst might happen.

All of my children are athletes and both of my boys play rugby. Seven years ago when my oldest son told me that he wanted to play rugby, I thought he was crazy. I was petrified, but I signed the consent despite my fears. All sports have a risk factor to them, but rugby is a high-risk rough and tough sport! At first, I was terrified. I had visions of my son getting seriously injured or even worse!

As time went on and I realized how much he loved the sport, I changed my way of thinking. Both of my boys have been seriously injured, but they still play the game. I don't fear the worst anymore. I hope for the best and wholeheartedly believe that if the worst did happen, they would be doing something they loved if it did happen.

You will notice on my S.W.O.F. analysis that most of my fears are associated with life-threatening outcomes. However, I also fear failure. I think that fear of failure is a universal fear. But if you change your way of thinking about failure, you can transform your weaknesses into strengths and realize opportunities for growth.

> IF I SUCCEED, I WIN! IF I FAIL, I LEARN! So either way, I WIN!

©2013 Comic Strip Mama Enterprises Inc.

Most times, fears will overwhelm you and stress you out when situations and circumstances arise that make it necessary to face them. Panic and frustration sets in and you tend to focus on the negative outcomes that may result because of your weaknesses.

Change your thinking and realize that there are positive lessons to be learned from any failure or negative outcome. If you fear for your life or the lives of others, you may have to reconsider taking certain risks. But you can't NOT cross the street because you might get hit by a car. If that's the way you live your life, you will never truly live.

Bottom line is...your weaknesses and fears should not cause you to BE weak and LIVE in fear!

STEP #15

Surround Yourself With People Who Bring Out the BEST in YOU!

©2013 Comic Strip Mama Enterprises Inc.

Relationships that you choose to build with people in life should bring out the absolute best in you continuously and genuinely...On good days when you are at your best and on bad days when you are at your worst. These relationships are the foundation of your life so it is super important to consider them very seriously.

People in this life will either bring out the BEST in YOU or the WORST. CHOOSE WISELY!

©2013 Comic Strip Mama Enterprises Inc.

Ultimately you want to choose awesome people that will love you, encourage you, stand up for you and stand beside you, even in the face of adversity. If certain people are constantly walking in and out of your life depending on the circumstances, then it's necessary to reconsider these relationships.

When choosing a life-partner, this is especially important. Before I met my "lover man", I was only ever interested in establishing a relationship to fill a lonely void and to help support me financially. I never thought about the long haul. I never *truly* considered compatibility or how a man should bring out the best in me and understand what was truly important to me. That was all secondary to not being lonely and the overwhelming feeling of not being strong enough financially to provide for my children and make it in life. I eventually realized that this is why my past relationships failed miserably. I didn't even know who I was or what was important to me in life, so how could I possibly expect to find a life partner that would have anything in common with me?

I finally took a relationship time-out to figure out who I was and what was important to me. I did struggle financially, but it wasn't the end of the world. I turned to my family and friends for help, made some temporary sacrifices and did what I had to do to go through this very important process.

This time-out was an awakening and I learned that I wasn't as lonely as I thought I was. I realized that I was already surrounded by a wealth of love and support from family and friends who brought out the best in me. So I focused on them and I focused on me.

Sometimes you have to take a TIME OUT to find yourself and figure things out!

©2013 Comic Strip Mama Enterprises Inc.

When I met my lover man, I didn't rush into anything. At first I wasn't really interested in a long-term relationship with him at all. But as I got to know me a little better and I got to know him a little better, I knew that we were perfect for one another. Since, we have established a strong and healthy relationship. I have realistic expectations of him and he has realistic expectations of me. And most importantly, we bring out the best in each other, despite the challenges we are faced with.

Any relationships you establish in life should be with people that ultimately bring out the best in you, intimate or platonic. You also need to find and surround yourself with people who you can let loose with, let your hair down with and blow off a little steam with! These people are an essential key element of your core life support system. When you find these awesome people, you must appreciate them and never take them for granted in order to keep them.

It is also important to remember that people should never be treated as possessions or obsessions. Healthy and strong relationships consist of **individuals** who are true to themselves, love themselves and respect themselves first. You should never be expected to stop being an individual in order to be in a relationship. If that's the case and you are miserable when a certain person in your life is not spending all of their free time focused on you or if a certain person acts miserably because you are not spending all of your free time focused on them, that is not a healthy relationship. It's an "obsessionship" and/or "possessionship"! These types of relationships are toxic and do not bring out the best in you continuously or genuinely! No one deserves to be treated that way.

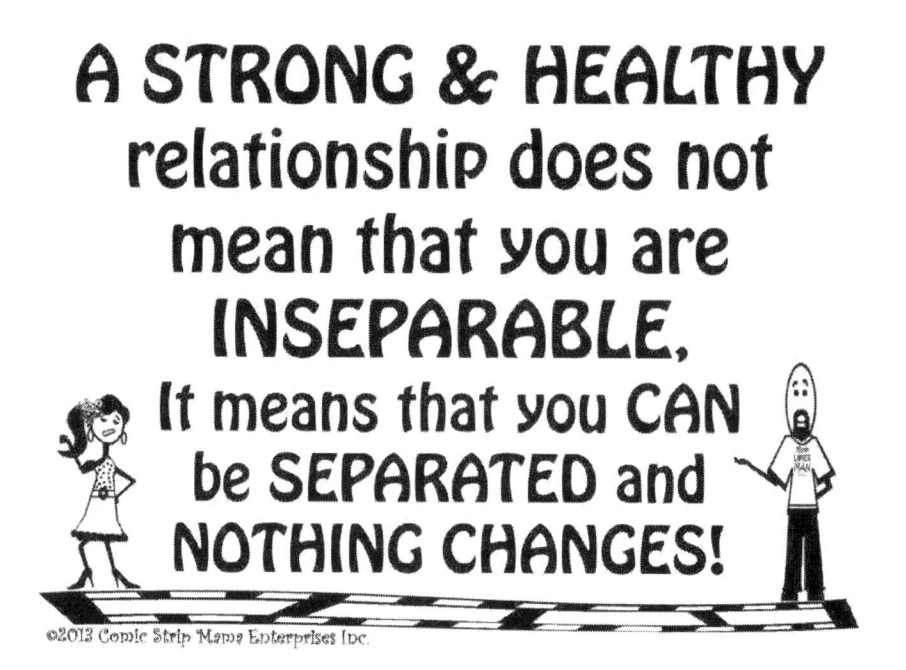

A STRONG & HEALTHY relationship does not mean that you are INSEPARABLE, It means that you CAN be SEPARATED and NOTHING CHANGES!

©2013 Comic Strip Mama Enterprises Inc.

So make an effort to build relationships and surround yourself with people that:

- Make you happy!
- Accept you, respect you and love you for you!
- Appreciate you and are grateful for you!

- Believe in you and realize your worth!
- Genuinely care about your best interest and well-being!
- Inspire you to be awesome!
- Keep you positive and motivated to good do things!
- Lift you up when you are feeling down!
- Make you smile and laugh when you feel like crying!
- Encourage you to keep it together even when you have every reason to fall apart!
- Use good judgement and have good morals and values!
- Are loving, compassionate and kind!
- Embrace positive change and have an open mind!

Do NOT surround yourself with people that:

- Do not respect you, accept you and make you sad.
- Take you for granted and use you.
- Only focus on the negative.
- Take you for granted.
- Don't inspire you or value your worth.
- Don't motivate you to be the best that you can be.
- Weigh you down and hold you back from being awesome.
- Bring you down so low you question your existence.
- Cause you to feel unnecessary negativity, anger and hatred.
- Cause toxic drama.
- Wallow in self-pity or cause you to wallow in self-pity.
- Physically and mentally abuse you or other people and things with their power.
- Use poor judgement and encourage reckless and self destructive behavior.
- Do not embrace positive change.

Surround yourself with people and things that are awesome, make you feel awesome, encourage you want to BE awesome and bring out all of the things that bring out the BEST in YOU!

STEP #16

Make Good LIFE Investments!

NOT the money kind!

©2013 Comic Strip Mama Enterprises Inc.

I'm not talking about the money kind of investments...I'm talking about life investments.

You should never do anything for anyone with the intention of getting something in return, unless it is your job and you are being compensated for it. I realize that it's nice to hope that people will recognize that you have done something for them and in turn, do something you, but EXPECTING them to will only set yourself up for disappointment more often than not. This, I have learned the hard way.

> Good LIFE INVESTMENTS happen when you stop thinking in terms of "what's in it for ME?!" and more in terms of "what's the return on investment?!"

©2013 Comic Strip Mama Enterprises Inc.

When you do something for someone, stop thinking in terms of "what's in it for me" and more in terms of "what's the return on investment". And that still doesn't mean that should expect that person to repay you. The return on investment might only be the satisfaction that you made a genuine positive effort and made a difference in someone else's life, because you could. Every positive effort we make in this life should be considered an intangible "investment". Your behavior and your actions should always in some way, add value to your life, to someone else's life or to the greater good of the universe as a whole.

Just like tangible investments, intangible investments can be risky. However, it doesn't necessarily mean you shouldn't make them. There is always a chance that you will invest more than you should and you will end up feeling burned, disappointed, angry, hurt and feeling sorry for yourself. But the most important thing is that you get to walk away knowing that you made a genuine positive effort. When you feel this way, feeling good about your efforts and learning positive lessons from the experience becomes your return on investment.

And yes, I do believe that you should save most of your positive energy and invest in the people that count and will in turn add some value to your life. However, sometimes doing something awesome for a person that you know will probably never return the favor or a person you know you will most likely never encounter again can have amazing positive effects. Positive energy is infectious and contagious. You never know when your positive efforts will turn a negative into a positive and result in a chain reaction. It's happening more and more these days and we hear about it all the time. So don't allow negativity to prevent you from doing unto others as you want KARMA to do unto you.

DO unto others as you'd have KARMA do unto YOU!

©2013 Comic Strip Mama Enterprises Inc.

If you keep giving and giving, and you get burned over and over again, then you must question your efforts and think about why you keep getting burned. Perhaps, you are being an enabler or a doormat? You should never allow yourself to be taken for granted, but in the same sense, you should never take for granted your ability to do good things freely and make good life investments.

STEP #17

Get ON That BUCKET LIST!

Every DAY you have a CHOICE...
Keep DREAMING about your DREAMS or GET UP and make your dreams HAPPEN!!

We all have dreams of being things, doing things and seeing things. Every morning that you wake up and you acknowledge that you are still alive and well, you should look at it as another opportunity to turn your dreams into reality and make every effort to do so!

So, what are your dreams and life goals? Who do you aspire to be, what do you aspire to do and what do you aspire to see before you expire? Or..."kick the bucket"!

Think about that for a minute.

Now let me ask you this. What would you be if money didn't exist and you could be anything you wanted to be professionally? What kind of things would you do, where would you travel and what would you see?

All of these answers should be on your "Bucket List"!

My BUCKET LIST!

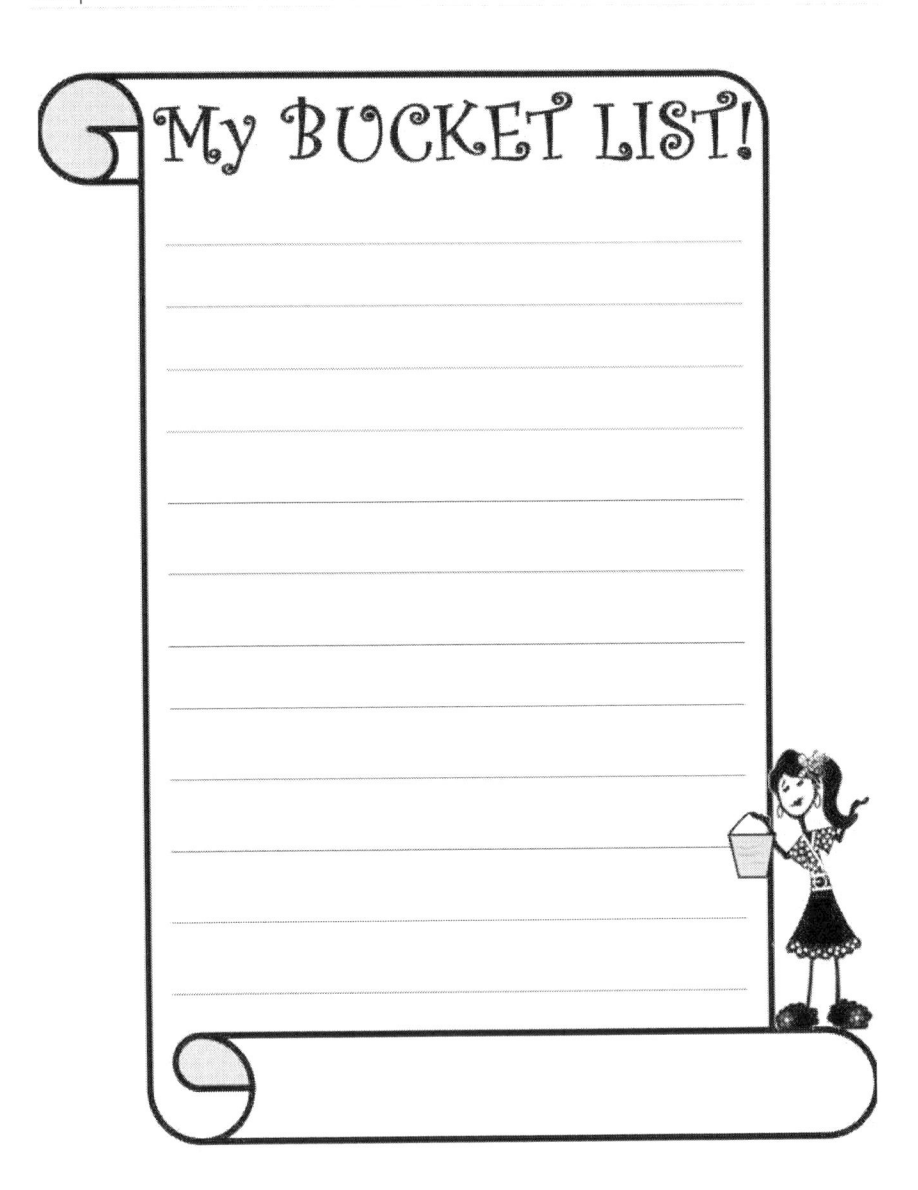

I know you are probably thinking that I'm crazy telling you to work towards achieving goals that might be really BIG dreams.

Well first of all, I'm insane...remember? And insane trumps crazy!

But in all seriousness, there is absolutely nothing wrong with dreaming big and then working towards making those dreams a reality! And I can tell you that these big dreams really can come true because I am making a really big dream happen for myself right now at this very moment!

I am encouraging and inspiring others to find the positive, the blessings and the humor in life and I am writing a book about all of it! I honestly didn't think I ever would be able to reach or help people on this level, because I could never afford the education to do so professionally. But guess what? I am doing it!

If you can DREAM IT... You can BE IT You can DO IT & You can SEE IT!

©2013 Comic Strip Mama Enterprises Inc.

You also need to establish some little goals too. Maybe some of your little goals can help you achieve some of the big goals.

If you don't have a written "bucket list", I strongly encourage you to start one. You can even print yourself one of my fancy shmancy bucket lists right off of the resources page on my website: (www.comicstripmama.com/resources)

Magnetize it to your fridge! You can also purchase one of my magnet white board bucket lists in my online store! =) Or, you can simply use a plain jane piece of paper. But whatever you do, make sure you post your bucket list somewhere you will see it regularly.

You can't plan for or make an effort to achieve your life goals until you have established some. So I really hope that you will make this step a priority!

Some more advice about making your dreams reality...If you don't know if you can do something, make sure you at least try...and give it 100% effort. Also, ask for help if you think someone can help you! You never know unless you ask and you have nothing to lose by asking.

And most importantly...

©2013 Comic Strip Mama Enterprises Inc.

STEP #18

Embrace Life Changes!

REINVENT yourself for YOU!

©2013 Comic Strip Mama Enterprises Inc.

I know this to be TRUE... YOU can only CHANGE for YOU!

©2013 Comic Strip Mama Enterprises Inc.

Change happens all around us and within us. It is an inevitable part of life and it is constant. Your response and willingness to change, on the other hand, is completely optional. Being able to embrace change, adapt in a positive way and reinvent yourself effectively is an essential life skill. Throughout the challenges of life you will experience involuntary life changes and voluntary life changes. These types of changes may include behavioural changes, lifestyle changes, body changes, habitual changes, habitat changes, social changes, spiritual changes, and so on.

Involuntary life changes are changes you are forced to consider due to circumstances and losses beyond your realm of control. They are the most difficult changes to make because you are not able to mentally prepare yourself for these sometimes tragic and unexpected situations.

Voluntary life changes are changes that you willingly make an effort to acknowledge, initiate and pursue. These types of changes are somewhat easier to embrace because you are making a conscious choice to change and you are able to mentally prepare yourself for the challenges you will face.

In any case, all change requires you to gather up all of the positive lessons, memories, people and things that you want to take with you as you change and leave the rest behind. Then you must step outside of your element and comfort zone and acknowledge, develop, transition and transform. In other words, you must recognize the *want* to change, set attainable goals to achieve the change, act on the plan to change, follow through with the change and then embrace the change and reinvent yourself! Notice how I said "***want***" and not "***need***"?

Here's the problem with change. Too many people try to change for the wrong reasons and either end up failing or living miserably just to make others happy.

Wanting to change and *needing* to change are two different things. You can acknowledge the *need* to change until you are blue in the face, but you need to *want* to change for the right reasons and the only right reason is for YOU. You can't change for your spouse, your family, your friends, not even for your children. They are very good reasons to change, but they should not be the only reason you want to change.

We all seek encouragement and validation when we embark on a journey to change. What usually happens when you change for other people is you announce that you are going to make a wonderful positive change and then you constantly seek the motivation and validation from the cheering squad. When you don't hear any cheering going on, you decide that the change is not worth the effort and you come to a screeching halt and start making excuses for not following through.

Allow me to illustrate the vicious cycle:

First this happens...

> **HEAR YEEEE... HEAR YE! I'm going to make a CHANGE! I'm really going to change for the better this time!**

WHY isn't anyone cheering?!?!

©2013 Comic Strip Mama Enterprises Inc.

And then...

> **HELLO? YOOO HOOOO! I'm over here, saying I'm going to MAKE A CHANGE!! Can I get a "That's AWESOME!"?!**

Maybe nobody heard ME?!?!

©2013 Comic Strip Mama Enterprises Inc.

And then....

> *This SUCKS! Why should I change?!?!*
>
> **HELLO? Doesn't ANYBODY care that I'm going to CHANGE?! ANYBODY??!! Not even the people I am changing for?!**

©2013 Comic Strip Mama Enterprises Inc.

And THEN...

> *Maybe I was changing for the WRONG reasons?!*
>
> **CHANGE SHMANGE! Why bother?! It's too hard and it's not worth the effort when NOBODY even cares that I SAID I was going to CHANGE!**

©2013 Comic Strip Mama Enterprises Inc.

Most times failure to follow through with change is a result of doing it for the wrong reasons. If you change for the right reason, because *you want* to change, then validation and motivation from other people shouldn't matter at all because you are not changing for them, you are changing for you! If all you care about is who's noticing what you are doing and cheering you on, take my advice and start over. YOU should be your biggest cheerleader in life.

I know how tough it can be to change and it is way easier when others support us and motivate us along the way. However, we all say things we don't follow through with from time to time. You must remember that actions speak louder than words. Saying and doing are two different things, but many of us expect the support, encouragement and validation from others to start immediately when we make this wonderful declaration that we are going to change for the better!

Once you start following through with your plan to change, your accomplishments are more likely to be acknowledged and you will naturally receive support, validation and encouragement, providing you have made an effort to surround yourself with people that bring out the best in you. If so, it will be genuine and effortless, not forced or fake.

Another thing to remember is that any significant change doesn't happen overnight and it takes some getting used to. You may even regress and fail along the way. Even when you trip and fall throughout your journey to change, you should be able to pick yourself back up again and keep on keepin' on. If you need a little time to breathe, reassess, mentally prepare or even grieve, take it! It's part of the change process. Just don't give up, blame others or make excuses for not following through.

I think that it's pretty obvious that I have had to deal with my fair share of involuntary and voluntary change throughout my lifetime and I struggled through a lot of it. I still struggle with voluntary self-improvement changes all the time! But when it comes to making significant life changes in the face of adversity and tragedy, I changed my way of thinking and being. As a result, I have found that I am able to easily acknowledge, develop, transition and transform in order to survive, no matter what life throws at me. It's like I automatically go into reinvention mode as soon as something happens. I start repairing, healing and changing immediately because I know it's necessary to live my life to the fullest. Most importantly, I make these changes for ME.

Life is much too short to waste time hemming and hawing and wallowing away in negativity and self-pity. When change is the only option, you must embrace change and choose to live an awesome life!

STEP #19

Open Your MIND!

> Challenge yourself to experience something new every day!

©2013 Comic Strip Mama Enterprises Inc.

©2013 Comic Strip Mama Enterprises Inc.

Although I believe that it is very important to be a strong minded person, I would never suggest that you live primarily inside your own mind.

We all have our own thoughts, our own tastes, our own likes, our own dislikes, our own experiences, our own knowledge, our own opinions and our own beliefs. We all look at the world through different eyes and think and interpret things with different minds. However, I strongly believe that you should not limit yourself and only exist within the confines of your own mind.

Closed minded people truly miss out on so much. They are often negative towards others and have a difficult time embracing change and accepting and respecting differences simply because they are not willing to give anything new or different a chance.

There is so much awesome diversity in the world! I am truly grateful for all of the people I have met, the opportunities that I have had, the knowledge that I have gained and the experiences I have enjoyed throughout my journey in life...simply because I have an open mind.

One of the things that I always point out to people who insist on not giving something or someone a chance, particularly when they are doing so because they associate it with something they consider bad or evil, is this...There is good and bad in EVERYTHING!

We can't negatively judge or condemn an entire group of things or an entire group of people just because there are things or people within that group that have been bad or evil. It is insane how often people do this. It is the main reason that this world is so messed up. It is the reason why so much hate exists.

It doesn't take a lot to open your mind, but it does take some effort to give new things and people a chance. If you can't give them a chance, just live and let live and mind your own. But, I strongly encourage you to open your mind, experience new things, meet new people and be willing to experience the diversity of life to the fullest!

STEP #20

STOP Taking Life WAY Too Seriously!!!

"Have a sense of HUMOR!!"

©2013 Comic Strip Mama Enterprises Inc.

You know what? Sometimes my age IS inappropriate for my behavior and I'm proud and purrrrfectly comfortable with that.

These days, I would say that I spend about 10% of my life taking it seriously and about 90% of my life laughing ALL the WAY to the grave!

Out of the 10% of seriousness, I would say that honestly, I probably spend about 5% taking life a little too seriously. But just a little. And that is mostly because I am a little paranoid and overreact about certain things that I really shouldn't be paranoid about. But I usually figure out that I'm overreacting fairly quickly.

Taking life a little seriously is necessary. Everything can't ALWAYS be humorous. We all have responsibilities and obligations and life isn't always fair, easy or fun.

You can be serious and people can take you seriously without being serious all of the time. Sometimes the challenges we face really suck. But these difficulties, obstacles and challenges shouldn't interfere with your ultimate enthusiasm for living life happily and to the fullest.

Some people take life WAY too seriously! I know. I used to be one of them. Mind you, that was back in the day, before I found Awesomeness. (B.A. = Before Awesomeness) But, not anymore! Nosirree! These days, if I can, you betcha I will find the humor in everything, if possible, as soon as possible.

> I am quite certain that if I lost my sense of HUMOR, it would most definitely need to be replaced by a PADDED CELL!

©2013 Comic Strip Mama Enterprises Inc.

I have absolutely no interest in wasting any more of my life being negative, angry, depressed or causing toxic drama. It's all a waste of time and energy.

Q. How do you stop taking life to seriously?

A. Simply by looking for the humor in everything.

There will be times when you can't find humor in some things and if that's the case, try not to cause unnecessary drama just because you aren't amused or you're easily offended.

People swear, talk about sex, say inappropriate things, laugh at inappropriate times, use sarcasm and some people might do things that you don't agree with. But if it's meant to be humorous and it's not evil or inflicting physical and/or mental pain, pay no mind to it. If it *really* bothers you, then there is nothing wrong with saying so, but in a respectful, non-dramatical way. Just because a person has a different sense of humor than you do, doesn't mean that they deserve to be disrespected.

Humor is a matter of style. We don't have to like someone else's sense of humor, but I think we should respect freedom of speech, as long as it's not evil, hateful or criminal.

There are so many different styles of humor that you may or may not relate to or care for. For example, some people think that my humor and my comics are distasteful because I talk about parents drinking. Some of these individuals have even gone so far as to suggest that I'm an alcoholic irresponsible mother and state that no parent who drinks alcohol could ever be a responsible one.

eye roll

If being a MOM who loves to enjoy some WINE from time to time is WRONG... Then I don't wanna be RIGHT!!

©2013 Comic Strip Mama Enterprises Inc.

Do I drink alcohol? Absolutely. It is one of my liquid sanities. (Coffee is the other!) But I always drink responsibly, like MILLIONS of other parents and adults in this world.

I know my limit and I drink within it and I'm an awesome mom regardless of what people might think. I also enjoy some liquid sanity with a lot of other awesome, responsible parents. I know that not everyone can handle drinking alcohol. My birth mother was one of them. But I can assure you that I have no issues with addiction to alcohol and most people who drink in moderation don't either. Most people drink alcohol to celebrate, relax, unwind and numb the insanity in their mind. And if doing so is wrong, then I don't wanna be right!

Too much of almost anything is not good for you. If something brings out the worst in you or you can't function without it, then you need to recognize that red flag.

End of vent!

Now back onto humor styles:

My style of humor is simple. I like to be sarcastic and witty...I may even say things that are a little inappropriate at times, but I try to think before I speak and I am mindful of where I am and who is around when I say certain things.

I choose not to swear excessively, but not because I never swear. I do swear sometimes, especially when I'm having a little vent session with one of my special ones. But I know who I can use certain humor with and I try really hard not to offend people. I am also mindful of the fact that I am building a business and a brand. I want to be seen as a positive public figure and role model. I don't want to be seen as a person with a "like it or suck it" attitude who doesn't give a shit (see, I swear) about what other people think and feel. Because I genuinely do care and I would rather change an angry negative person into a happy positive person and make them laugh instead of get all get all pissed off and telling them where to go. And, if all else fails, I always have laughter, sarcasm and vent sessions with my special ones to keep me comfortably insane. ;)

We all come from a different walk of life that ultimately shapes our sense of humor and I do enjoy all different styles....even some "inappropriate" humor. I will admit that some people definitely cross the line when it comes to their sense of humor and behavior, but like I have said before...There is good and bad in everything!

If you don't find something funny, ask yourself if it's worth taking time and energy to make a judgement call. Otherwise, just live and let live.

The bottom line is we ALL need to laugh throughout the challenges of life! Instead of taking life way too seriously, find the humor in it whenever possible and laugh out loud!

Laugh at yourself, laugh at others and encourage others to do the same. Laughter is the cheapest, safest, most awesome form of medicine on the face of the earth, so overdose on it!

LAUGHTER is a gateway drug to AWESOMENESS
©2013 Comic Strip Mama Enterprises Inc.

STEP #21

Respect and Accept Differences!

> Make GOOD judgements!

©2013 Comic Strip Mama Enterprises Inc.

> **In life, the only TRUE DISABILITY is our INABILITY to ACCEPT & RESPECT DIFFERENCES!**
>
> ©2013 Comic Strip Mama Enterprises Inc.

Are you wasting part of your life negatively judging others' looks, behaviour, choices, opinions, beliefs and lifestyle simply because they look different, speak differently, act differently, dress differently, choose differently, think differently, believe differently or love differently than you do?

It amazes me how many people insist on wasting precious time and energy negatively judging differences when ALL people on the planet ARE different. There is no such thing as a "normal" person and as long as a person is not doing anything *truly* harmful or evil, it should not make a difference how different they are. Instead, everyone should be accepted and respected for who they are, no matter how different they may be.

If you noticed, I said: "As long as a person is not doing anything *truly* **harmful or evil**, it shouldn't make a difference how different they are." I would never suggest that anyone should respect and accept people that are harmful or evil. But what is your interpretation of harmful and evil? That is a complicated loaded question that I'm not going to elaborate on. I will, however, explain to you what my interpretation is.

Basically, if you are not a compulsive liar, a cheater, a backstabber, a user, a criminal, a mental/physical abuser or a murderer, you are good in my books and I will respect you and accept you for the person you are. It's that simple.

If a person is any of the above and they affect my life or the lives of the people I love negatively in some way, I will never tolerate, respect or accept these evil differences and you can be sure that I will stand up and speak up. You can call it judgement if you want, but I call it good, positive and sound judgement. This type of judgement is fair and absolutely necessary to protect yourself and the ones you love.

Otherwise, the way I see it is, I don't have to like someone or agree with someone in order to respect and accept their differences. I may even like and agree with certain things about a person and dislike and disagree with certain things about the same person.

I'm not going to lie, sometimes I think that certain differences are crazy, outrageous or humorous. But who am I to negatively judge them? If I see a good and positive judgement call opportunity, I might take it if I think I genuinely can help someone and I truly have their best interest at heart. If I have nothing good to offer, then I mind my own and let others do as they do and be who they be.

I strongly encourage you to open your mind and live the same way. I have encountered so many fascinating, awesome and unique people in this life and it's really true what they say, "You can't judge a book by its cover"! You need to take a good look at what's inside and sometimes you might even need to get past the first few chapters to really have a good understanding.

Remember, we all walk a different path in life and for the most part, people genuinely have good intentions and strive to be good, honest people. Just because someone isn't walking on the same path as you are, it doesn't mean they aren't headed in the same direction...it's just a different way.

Hey! I'm going to take THIS PATH!
I'm going to take THIS PATH! See you there!
Awesomeville!
©2013 Comic Strip Mama Enterprises Inc.

STEP #22

Don't Measure Success in Dollars & Cents!

©2013 Comic Strip Mama Enterprises Inc.

©2013 Comic Strip Mama Enterprises Inc.

Being successful in life should never be measured by how much money you have in your bank account or by the material things that you possess. If this book was about business success, then yes, money would most definitely be a factor. But, it's not. This book is about life.

I am not successful in life, as a person or a parent or even as an entrepreneur because I am rolling in lots of dough or have the best of everything. No, no, noooo. Not even close. I am successful in life because I am a strong, positive, happy, awesome person who makes an effort to positively impact, empower and add value to the lives of others every chance I get. I am also successful because of my skills, knowledge, experience, my open mind and my ability to make good choices. I take great pride in all of it.

I could have stayed on the path of reckless behaviour and self-destruction, but I didn't. I made a choice to make peace with my past, accept accountability and change my way of thinking about life. I made a choice to stop setting myself up for failure, stop thinking negatively and instead find the positive, the blessings and the humor in everything. Then I made a choice to put myself out there, encourage others to do the same and lead by example.

If you have made a choice to read this book, then I'm going to guess that you also have the mental ability to also make all of the same types of choices. One of the main reasons I have been so successful is I decided to embrace the power of the World Wide Web and social media. It is incredible how many people you can reach and lives you can impact in a positive way, as a result. Some weeks I reach millions!

I encourage you to take a really good look at your life and measure how successful you are at this moment. Remember, nothing is ever going to be perfect. You can't strive for perfection because striving for perfection is impossible. But you can strive to be the best, most awesome person you can be.

STEP #23

Take Time for Yourself, Take Care of Yourself & Reward Yourself!

©2013 Comic Strip Mama Enterprises Inc.

> It is NOT selfish to take time for yourself, take care of yourself and REWARD YOUSELF! It is absolutely NECESSARY and important!

©2013 Comic Strip Mama Enterprises Inc.

It makes me sad when I hear people say that they don't have time to take time for themselves, take care of themselves and/or reward themselves. I often hear this from working parents, single parents, caregivers and entrepreneurs.

Living a full life is hard and it's extremely challenging, especially when you have multiple priorities. However, only focusing on *other* people and *other* things and not yourself will eventually send you into a tailspin of burnout! Eventually you will become overwhelmed, exhausted, annoyed and frustrated.

If you believe that taking time to focus on yourself is selfish, I want you to change your way of thinking immediately! The truth is, taking time for yourself is necessary, very important and it is essential for your mental health.

If everyone in your life is used to you doing and being everything to everyone ALL of the time, you need to sit down with them and have a little chitty chat. Communication is super important. You need to tell the people in your life that you are going to start taking time to focus on yourself. Schedule it if you have to! Ask for help if you need to!

Ideally, you should take time to focus on *just* yourself at least once a day, even if it's only for a few minutes. And this could be doing something as simple as doing nothing at all except for relaxing, thinking and de-stressing. It's good to do nothing at all from time to time! It's not selfish, so stop thinking it is.

©2013 Comic Strip Mama Enterprises Inc.

Taking care of yourself physically and mentally is also super important. This is when you will take time to enhance your beauty and get spiffed up every now and then. You might also focus on improving your physical and mental health by exercising more, meditating, eating healthy and taking time to talk and vent with a special one.

Rewarding yourself comes next. You must take a little bit of time out of life to acknowledge your accomplishments and hard work and reward yourself for them! I'm not suggesting that you run out and spend a whole whack of money on yourself, but you could spend some.

If you have some disposable income, think about taking a little getaway. Maybe you could buy yourself a new pair of shoes you have been admiring for some time or buy some new clothes. Perhaps you could get a manicure or a pedicure or get your hair done professionally. You could eat out and let someone else cook, clean and wait on you for a change. You could spend time working on a hobby. Whatever you do to reward yourself, make sure you DO something that makes you feel good, because you deserve it!

If you don't have disposable income, no problem! Your reward could be as simple as taking some uninterrupted time to read a good book, taking a cat nap or taking a nice hot bubble bath and pampering yourself. But make sure you turn off the world while you are rewarding yourself.

You deserve to celebrate and reward yourself every now and then for the things you have accomplished in every aspect of your life! ;)

STEP #24

Do Random Acts of Awesomeness!

> And BE PROUD of it!!

©2013 Comic Strip Mama Enterprises Inc.

Kindness, generosity and compassion are super important things to practice in this life. Random acts of awesomeness are probably the most rewarding things that you will do in your lifetime. (Unless you are a parent, then being a parent is probably the most rewarding.) But in any case, you are giving a part of yourself selflessly.

I have often heard the phrase "work for a cause and not for applause". When I first heard this phrase, I was in complete agreement. But the more I thought about it, the more I felt that there was something not quite right about that phrase.

While I agree that you should never do anything for another person expecting something from *them* in return, I do not think that there is anything wrong with being proud of doing awesome things and being recognized for them. So I have changed this phrase slightly:

Ahhh, yes... THAT'S better!

WORK for a CAUSE and NOT ~~ONLY~~ for APPLAUSE!

©2013 Comic Strip Mama Enterprises Inc.

The more we talk about the awesome things that we do, the more we encourage others to do the same types of awesome things. There is absolutely nothing wrong with being proud about doing kind, generous and compassionate things for others just as long as your intentions are genuine and not solely for self-recognition.

Could you imagine if we all stayed silent about these things? No one would ever make an effort to do anything kind and awesome. Especially children! Children thrive on recognition and acknowledgement for the awesome things that they do, but so do adults and there is nothing wrong with that.

I think it's extremely important and necessary to recognize others for the amazing and awesome things that they do and I think that it's equally important to receive recognition for the amazing and awesome things that you do!

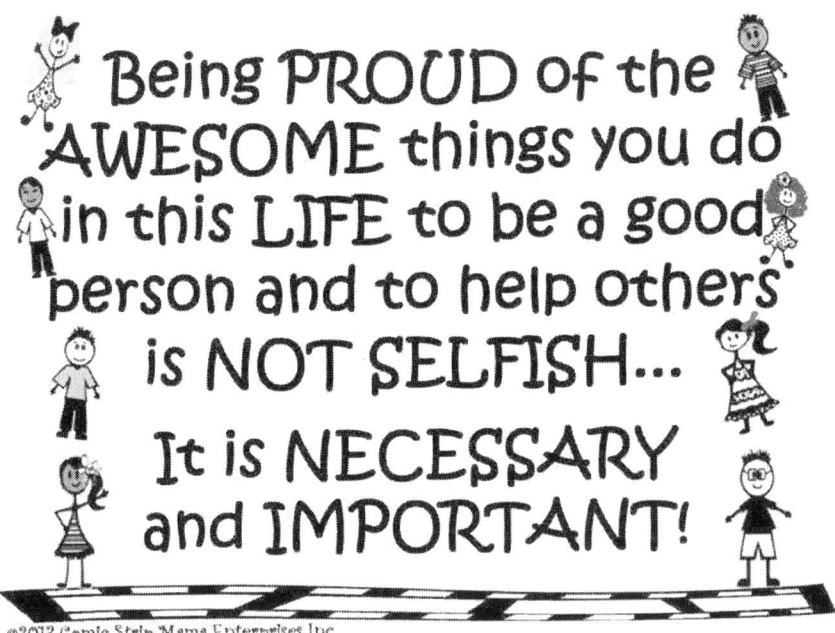

> **Being PROUD of the AWESOME things you do in this LIFE to be a good person and to help others is NOT SELFISH... It is NECESSARY and IMPORTANT!**
>
> ©2013 Comic Strip Mama Enterprises Inc.

Being kind, generous and compassionate does take some effort, but not a lot. Acts of awesomeness can be things that are simple and they don't even need to cost a cent. Kind words and gestures can go a long way, brighten up a person's day and make the world a better, more positive place. When you practice doing these things often enough, they become second nature.

Make sure you make an honest effort to greet and acknowledge people you encounter on a daily basis. Make eye contact, SMILE, say hi and ask them how they are. Have a little chitty chat and a little laugh if you can. When someone does something for you, even if they are being paid to do it, say please and thank you. When a person thanks you, acknowledge that you appreciate it.

A SMILE is understood In ANY Language

©2013 Comic Strip Mama Enterprises Inc.

Make sure you compliment people and help them realize and acknowledge their worth. Tell them how awesome they are despite their flaws and differences. If someone is down on themselves, cheer them up, make them laugh and lift their spirits. If you are comfortable doing it, give that someone a hug if they need it.

When you practice these things, really pay attention to the reactions of other people around you. You will notice that a lot of times you will influence the way others treat people in a positive way, simply by doing awesome positive things.

If you are more fortunate than others, then give a little bit of that to people who are less-fortunate. I know you can only give what you can afford to give, physically, mentally and monetarily. But sometimes you can go a little bit beyond your means and give a little more than you should. It is important and necessary to give what you can, when you can, and recognize a need to do so. Can you imagine how awesome life would be if everyone made an effort to do these things? I can.

STEP #25

Give Yourself Regular Reality Checks!

Take time to LOOK BACK!

©2013 Comic Strip Mama Enterprises Inc.

Well my friend, congratulations. You have reached the 25th Step and you are well on your way to living a life of awesomeness! But no matter how awesome you are or how awesome your life is, there will be times that you will slip on some of these steps.

No one is perfect and sometimes life and people are cruel and vicious. No matter how positive you are, how awesome you are, how successful you are and no matter how hard you try to prevent it, LIFE will throw you some blinding curveballs out of nowhere, when you least expect it! Some of the difficulties, obstacles and tragedies that these curveballs present may seem insurmountable, especially at first. I know. I have faced my fair share of seemingly insurmountable curveballs throughout the challenges of my life!

So what do you do when life throws you a curveball? You must accept accountability and deal with it. Don't run away from it, duck or try to dodge it. Don't swing and strike out or even "throw it back hard". Doing any of that shifts blame and accountability. The only right thing to do is catch it and deal with it.

When life throws you a curveball, there is usually a reason it is being thrown at you. If there is not an apparent reason, there are usually not-so-apparent life lessons and blessings to be found and you need to try really hard to recognize them. You also need to try and find some humor if possible.

Reality checks are very important and another aspect of giving yourself a reality check is making sure you take time to look back and assess.

Yes, I'm telling you to look back at the past. And yes, I realize that most people will tell you to "leave the past behind you" or "forget about the past" or "don't look back". Well, I'm strongly encouraging you to ignore all of that advice. I'm not suggesting that you should *live* in the past, but you definitely need to look back at the past, for several reasons.

I know sometimes it's hard to look back there. But your past, good or bad, is what ultimately shapes you into the person you are today. If you don't look back at the past from time to time, how are you ever going to remember the awesome times? How are you going to help others learn from what you have lived? And most importantly, how are you going to realize everything that you have learned and prove how far you've come? You can't do any of that if all you focus on is now and the future.

> *You* **MUST** *look back at the* **PAST** *to* **REMEMBER** *the* **AWESOME** *times, to help someone* **LEARN** *from what you have* **LIVED,** *to* **REALIZE** *what you have* **LEARNED** *and to* **PROVE** *how far* **YOU** *have* **COME***!*

STEP #26

Believe in Something LARGER than LIFE!

©2013 Comic Strip Mama Enterprises Inc.

©2013 Comic Strip Mama Enterprises Inc.

Like I have stated time and again throughout this book, I don't care who or what you believe in and I will never ever negatively judge anyone for their spiritual and cultural beliefs, as long as they are not evil, hurtful, hateful or criminal.

There are aspects to many religions and cultures that I absolutely agree with and there are aspects that I absolutely do not agree with. I will not elaborate on these things in this book. However, I will say that I am the type of person that wholeheartedly believes that every person on the face of the earth should believe in something larger than life and exactly what that is should be a person's individual choice. I know that not all of you reading this will agree with that and I respect that.

I am an open minded multi-spiritual person. I believe in a lot of different things and I am always open to learning new things about spirituality. Ultimately, I believe that all people should just try their very best to be good, honest, kind, compassionate, generous and grateful. I believe that all people should respect and accept others and live in harmony. I believe that when the power of love, laughter and positivity overcomes the love of power, anger and negativity, the world will be a better place.

I do not necessarily believe in heaven or hell per se. I believe in "spirits" and a higher power. I believe that when we die, we cross over into a place that far surpasses anything this earth has to offer and our energy transforms from human form to a more powerful, immoral spiritual form that can travel anywhere in the universe. I believe that when we become this form, we have the power to watch over and protect our special ones here on earth.

I also believe in KARMA.

> Welcome to the KARMA CAFE! There are NO menus... You get what you DESERVE!

©2013 Comic Strip Mama Enterprises Inc.

Yep! I believe that everything happens for a reason. I believe that what goes around comes around. I believe when it's your time to die, it's your time. And I believe that Karma is the force behind all of it.

Believing in Karma gives me hope that everyone will eventually get what they deserve, good or bad, and that keeps me focused on being a good person and making wise choices.

HA! Just sayin'!

STEP #27

Enjoy Life, Have Fun and Socialize MORE!

©2013 Comic Strip Mama Enterprises Inc.

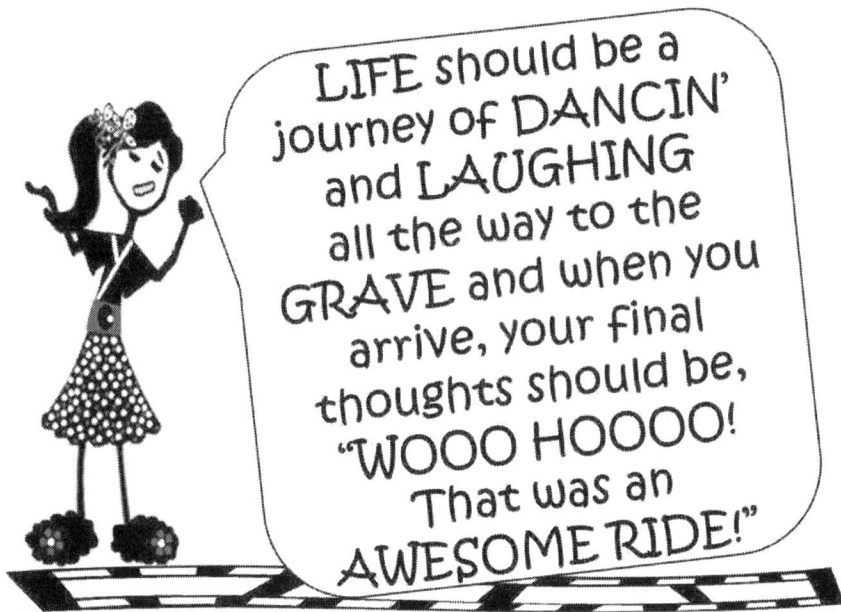

> "LIFE should be a journey of DANCIN' and LAUGHING all the way to the GRAVE and when you arrive, your final thoughts should be, 'WOOO HOOOO! That was an AWESOME RIDE!'"

©2013 Comic Strip Mama Enterprises Inc.

I want you to think about your life journey up to this very moment. Would you say that you are *just* existing or would you say that you are actually making an honest effort to enjoy the ride?

If you are not enjoying life, having fun and spending quality time enjoying the company of others, you are not living life to the absolute fullest.

Life can't be all work and no play and it certainly can't be all about the serious stuff. It also can't be all about doing things for others and nothing for yourself. There must be a healthy balance of all of it and you should be loving and enjoying most of it. If you aren't doing this, then I strongly encourage you to make an effort to change that.

Remember...

So make an effort to get out there and start living it up!

STEP #28

Make the MOST of EVERY MOMENT!

Celebrate!

©2013 Comic Strip Mama Enterprises Inc.

Don't you wish that you had more time sometimes? I know I do!

Time is constant and you never know when it will run out. You can't slow time down or speed it up, but you can choose to make the most of it.

All too often we take time for granted. We are all guilty of it. We put things off, we put people off and sometimes we simply waste time doing unimportant things instead of putting time to good use. Taking a little "downtime" and time for yourself is necessary, but you should really try not to take time or your ability to make good use of time for granted.

Try not to waste time and let life pass you by. Value time and respect it. Value and respect your own time and value and respect other people's time. Time is something you can't get back once it has passed. Make sure you remember that. You might be able to make up for it, but there is no guarantee. So your best bet is to really try to make the best of every single moment, in the moment.

How do you make the most of every moment?

Well, I'm going to ask you to think about your eulogy again. What would you want it to say about how you spent your time on this earth? Think long and hard about that and then live that!

You see, one of the most important things about life to remember is, people cannot live forever, but memories can. You must make it a priority to value every moment of your time, celebrate and cease every opportunity to create awesome memories that will live on and on, even after you are gone.

STEP #29

Find the Positive Lessons, the Blessings & the Humor in Adversity!

©2013 Comic Strip Mama Enterprises Inc.

Adversity happens and it can strike you like a bolt of lightning!

A death of a special one, a life-threatening illness, a loss of physical or mental abilities, a terrible tragic accident, a failed relationship, a job loss, a crime, a betrayal, a severe consequence, a natural disaster or an act of war.

These tragic and sometimes seemingly insurmountable situations and circumstances can happen throughout the challenges of your life. They may be a caused by unforeseeable events that you have absolutely no control over, choices you have made or by someone else's actions.

When adversity strikes, you may feel overwhelming uncontrollable emotions of panic, shock, pain, suffering, negativity, anger, vengeance, sadness, confusion and self-pity. Remember, grief is a natural part of the grieving healing process. It's ok to feel all of these emotions temporarily, but they should never become a way of life.

In the face of adversity, you have three choices. You can let it can let it define you, destroy you or you can let it strengthen you. The outcome is up to you. If you choose to wallow in the sea of negative grieving emotions, you will eventually drown in it and you might even take others down with you. That isn't fair to yourself or anyone else.

> *In the face of* **ADVERSITY** *you have three choices, you can* **let it DEFINE** *you,* **let it DESTROY** *you,* **OR** *let it* **STRENGTHEN YOU!**
>
> ©2013 Comic Strip Mama Enterprises Inc.

So how do you let adversity strengthen you? Well, I have determined that there are seven important steps.

First, you need to be prepared! Adversity is an inevitable part of life. I'm not suggesting that you live your life in fear, but I am suggesting that you live your life expecting the worst and hoping for the best. As much as it might suck, bad things are going to happen regardless of your preparedness. However, being somewhat prepared does help strengthen you faster when you are faced with adversity.

Second, you must grieve. Do not ignore the pain! Feel the emotions, let them out and eventually release them. But try really hard not to release them in a negative way. You still must think before you speak and act. You still must accept accountability for your words, your actions and your behavior. You don't want to hurt others or compromise your well-being as a result. Turn to the people in your life who love and care for you and/or seek professional help if you feel the need to. Make good use of this time. It's your time to cry and let it all out.

Third, you must come to terms with adversity. This is the pivotal part of the process. For so long I just spun in circles trying to come to terms with the adversity I was faced with in my life simply because I was told that in order to come to terms with the bad and tragic things, I *had* to forgive and forget and learn to trust again. So I would try really hard to do just that. Then, I would struggle and struggle and struggle. Until eventually, I would regress into the grieving process until I hit rock bottom. Remember when I talked about excessive negative self-pity and depression, well that's how it happens. When you keep going back to it because you can't get past this point.

Remember, you don't have to forgive anybody, you don't have to forget anything and you never have to trust anyone fully. Most times it is impossible and that is why so many people have a difficult time coming to terms with adversity.

You must accept, learn and choose to continue to live. You need to accept the things that you cannot change. Then, you must recognize and focus on the positive lessons. Instead of wallowing in the "should haves", "would haves" and "could haves", you need to take advantage of the opportunity to learn from all of those things. There are positive lessons to be learned from everything. You just have to make an effort to find them. Then, you must choose to make an honest effort to make peace with the past and keep on living.

Fourth, you must take a good look around you. Take a good look at what's left and most importantly, who's left. Start with yourself. These are all blessings. Be grateful for them! No matter what adversity you are faced with in life, if you are alive and well, there is a reason for that. Believe that. Don't neglect what's left. Don't push everything and everybody away. Adversity can bring people closer together and open the door to new opportunities. You need to allow that to happen.

Fifth, find the humor in everything. No matter what adversity I am faced with in life, I will always try to find the humor in it! It is a coping skill that many people frown upon, yet it is one of the most essential. Most times when something tragic happens, you are not the only one who suffers as a result. Remember that. Being able to laugh at the insanity of life not only helps you heal, it helps others heal and it helps others help you heal. Here are some examples:

When my step-mother found out she had cancer, it was devastating. But she didn't let it devastate her or allow her family to feel devastated. Instead, she laughed about it every chance she could. When she had her breast removed, we all joked about how she could get a new and improved boob! She never did go for reconstruction surgery, so we still laugh about it.

When my oldest son almost died and he needed to have emergency surgery to remove his appendix, my father was on his death bed and I just gave birth to baby Lexie twelve days before it happened. Needless to say, I was an emotional train wreck. I was breast feeding and they wouldn't let me bring my baby into the hospital to feed because of the SARS outbreak. My son was petrified of needles and proceeded to lock himself in the washroom to avoid the IV, despite his severe pain. Then the nurses had to force him out of the washroom and rush him into surgery and in the meantime I was crying and leaking everywhere! When my son was in the OR I asked a nurse if there was a breast pump I could use. She left and returned with a huge mechanical contraption on a pole, on wheels. I just looked at her like she had two heads. I laughed out loud and asked her how I use it. She told me she wasn't sure, but indicated that there was a manual (the size of a novel) chained to the side of it that I could read, then she shrugged her shoulders and left. I remember reading the first paragraph then the next thing I knew, I woke up drenched in breast milk.

When my father was battling his terminal illness, in between the moments of seriousness and sadness, we laughed and joked about everything from getting botched blood transfusions to getting a liver transplant. I can honestly say that he laughed his way to the grave until his brain was poisoned and his ability to laugh was taken away. But up until that point, humor kept him alive and helped everyone cope.

When I had to have emergency surgery to remove a gigantic hemorrhagic ovarian cyst, my gynaecologist (who I had known for over 13 years at this point) was at my bedside when I came to in the recovery room. He apologized and told me very sincerely that he tried, but he could not save my ovary. The first thing out of my mouth was "how fast am I going to start growing a moustache?!" It hurt like hell, but I laughed out loud. Then he laughed out loud, shook his head and said that he could always count on me to find something funny about anything.

I will stop there, but I could probably go on and on and on and on and write an entire book on how I have found humor in all of the adversity that I have faced in life. The ability to laugh when you have every reason to break down and cry is a remarkable skill. Practice it.

Sixth, you must reinvent yourself into a stronger person. What doesn't kill you makes you stronger, right? Well that is not necessarily true. You have to want to make it a reality. You must *choose* to be a stronger, better person. You can choose to stay focused on the negative grieving emotions and change for the worse OR you can choose to focus on the positive lessons, the blessings and the humor and change for the better. But that choice is ultimately up to you. No matter what happens, always remember that you are stronger than you think you are.

Seventh, you must look back! You need to look back, assess your life and your relationships and acknowledge how far you've come. You must be proud of those accomplishments and celebrate them!

If you noticed, all of these steps have been discussed in other steps throughout this book. Perhaps now you see how important they are and why they are essential and fundamental. Adversity is a part of life and it can depress you, break you or strengthen you. If you practice living a life of awesomeness, adversity will be much easier to face and overcome.

STEP #30

BE an AWESOME Role Model!

I'm strong!
I'm positive!
I'm happy!
I'm smart!
I'm worth it!
I'm AWESOME and YOU can BE awesome too!

©2013 Comic Strip Mama Enterprises Inc.

A role model is someone whose behaviour and actions are admired and imitated by others. Being an awesome role model doesn't mean that you need to be perfect. I consider myself to be an awesome role model and I am far from perfect. If anything, being an awesome role model means that you realize that "real" people are not perfect and "perfect" people are not real.

"REAL" People are NOT perfect and "PERFECT" People are NOT REAL!!

©2013 Comic Strip Mama Enterprises Inc.

Quite frankly, people who *think* they are perfect really make my eyes roll back in my head!

If you make an honest effort to follow and practice all of the steps that I have outlined in this book, and encourage, inspire and empower others to do the same, you will be an awesome role model!

So realize that life is hard, expect it to be and embrace the insanity of it all.

Get over yourself, give yourself an attitude adjustment and learn how to react and think before you speak!

Learn who you really are, discover your purpose and self-worth. Then be yourself, love yourself and respect yourself!

Forget about everything you have learned about forgiving, forgetting, and trust. Instead, accept, learn and trust reasonably.

Accept accountability for your words, your actions and your behaviour.

Stop setting yourself up for failure and lower your expectations of yourself.

Assume nothing and form your own opinions.

Release anger, negativity and toxic drama.

Get over your false sense of entitlement. Feel grateful, not entitled and live simply within your means.

Don't succumb to your weaknesses and fears! Change your way of thinking about them.

Surround yourself with people that bring out the best in you and realize what that is.

Make good life investments and stop thinking in terms of "what's in it for me?" and more in terms of "what's the return on investment?"!

Get on that "bucket list" and make your dreams reality!

Embrace life changes and reinvent yourself every chance you get!

Open your mind and challenge yourself to experience something new every day!

STOP taking life WAY too seriously!

Respect and accept differences and make good judgements!

Don't measure success in dollars and cents. Measure it by time well spent!

Take time for yourself, take care of yourself and reward yourself because you deserve it!
Do random acts of awesomeness and be proud of it!

Give yourself regular reality checks and look back!

Believe in something larger than life.

Enjoy life, have fun and socialize more.

Make the most of every moment!

Find the blessings, the positive lessons and the humor in adversity.

And last, but certainly not least, make every effort to practice all of these steps and be an awesome role model!

THANK YOU & Conclusion

Words cannot properly express how truly grateful I am that you have taken precious time out of your life to read my book.

Thank you! Thank you! THANK YOU!

> Thank YOU!! THANK YOU!! I couldn't POSSIBLY thank you ENOUGH!!

©2013 Comic Strip Mama Enterprises Inc.

I hope that my life story and these fundamental steps that I have shared with you will encourage, inspire and empower you to stop taking life so seriously. I hope that now you will focus on the positives, the blessings and the humor in life and ultimately change your way of thinking and being.

"Awesomeness" is the closest thing to perfection that a human being can possibly achieve. Awesomeness encompasses strength, happiness, success, purpose and self-worth — all of the things we so desperately seek throughout our journey of life. Once you achieve awesomeness, you will discover that it is the only way to live life to the absolute fullest.

Reinventing yourself and achieving awesomeness is not easy. There are many challenges, obstacles and fears that you will face along the way. Don't let them discourage you. Just take one step at a time and enjoy the climb!

Take ONE step at a time and ENJOY the CLIMB!
STAIRWAY to
Awesomeness!

Some Acknowledgements of the STUFF That Makes It WORTHWHILE!

Comments from readers:

YOU CAN DO IT!!

I am SO GRATEFUL and SO BLESSED to have some of the BEST READERS EVER!!

©2013 Comic Strip Mama Enterprises Inc.

"I fell in love with Comic Strip Mama from the moment I saw her first comic, and it was her first. Been a huge fan since the beginning and I am planning on continuing to support her. :)" —Joshua G.

"I can't wait until your first book comes out! As one devoted FAN, I'll definitely buy a copy or two! I just hope that one day, a book tour or something brings you this far South so I can meet you in person, and let you know just HOW MUCH your comics and conversations mean to me! Love you "Mama"!!! Keep up the good work! I can't wait to see what you come up with next!!" —Carla H. W.

"You are absolutely wonderful! I wish there were more people in this world like you!" —Shannon M.

"Mama, (feels so weird calling you that—since you are a gazillion years younger than me - but your wisdom & empathy is astounding). Have been faithfully watching all your posts & wishing u all the best in your ventures. You will be a huge success. Please keep up your posts. You are truly an inspiration. XXXX" —Kelly I.

"Thank you for working so hard to bring love and laughter to a sad world! You spread joy and inspiration with fairness, firmness, justice and good humor so you will never fail. God Bless your family and efforts!" —Meemaw K.

"You are an awesome inspiration. I read you, I read in some lines my life. I simply love you. And if you are planning on writing a book, I will buy it and give a copy to every negative, drama person I know, but please make your history the introduction to it, so everyone can appreciate the beauty of it and realize that is not one comic or book more, it is a therapy for life without the hassle of the $80.00 cost visits." —Martha G.

"I am new to your site. I found you through a friend and love your style! You put a smile on my face and make me laugh. To me, that's priceless! Thank you! :-)" —Wendy L.

"AMAZING!! I am a single mom of 4 awesome teens and we all LOVE to read your comics! My kids swear you can read my mind LOL! Coffee is my 2nd love after my kiddos. I know if my day isn't going so well I can click on your page and I will giggle and smile. Thank you so much from all of us here." —Tracy

"I'm one of the many man fans on her Facebook page that love her inspiration quotes, witty humor, liquid sanity and the "For the Love of...." comics. I always look forward coming home from work and catch up on the latest episode of Comic Strip Mama. :) To life, love, laughter and liquid sanity :)" —Steven J.

"When I get on FB, these are the post I look for first. I share them with my friends and they love them too. Don't stop believing in laughter....!!! It soothes the soul." —Pam W.

"As a Mom it gets crazy a lot in my house and it can make me go a little insane. But no sooner than logging into my Facebook, my mood immediately is changed just by reading your updated status. To me Facebook needs you & so do I and others. Thank you Comic Strip Mama for posting all your fabulous & funny comics." —Maryellen

"You are truly blessed and amazing! Thank you for sharing your gift! You have made my days. Your strips put laughter in my soul!" —Amy

"YOU ROCK!!! You take the daily stresses that we can all relate to and turn it into laughter, like no other...the kind of thing that gets me through the day. If people could learn to do this, we would finally have world peace..." —Crystal

"You always make me smile and laugh and you are also very real about important issues and I respect and appreciate you so much. When I first found your page, I was going through a very hard home situation and just reading your posts and your strips made me keep a little piece of happiness inside me when I was at a point when I had no hope for my future and the horrible man I was with. He was very abusive and a huge bully. I just want to thank you from the bottom of my now healing heart. Keep on being amazing! —Sara J.

"I love that you write about ordinary people, flaws as well as good points. It's great to know that we all share the same ups and downs in this life. You bring a smile to my face every day, even when it's not going so good. I look forward to your daily renderings and sharing them with my friends. You're an inspiration! Keep doing what you're doing....it's working!!!" —Christina L.

"Whenever I am going thru crap in my life you make it easier by not only putting a smile on my face but making me laugh and reminding me that we are all in this together!!!" —Sonya

Allow ME to Introduce the Comic Cast!

Meet MY Awesome FAMILY!

©2013 Comic Strip Mama Enterprises Inc.

I am truly blessed and I am so incredibly grateful to have such an amazing awesome family!

Meet MY Mamas In Crime!

Mamasita and her family! Gramma! Baby Mama! Dollie Mama! The Creelmama! Wise Mama!

©2013 Comic Strip Mama Enterprises Inc.

The Mamasita is a character based on my sister-in-love, my brother, my beautiful niece and nephew and their little dog Bailey! My sister in love is an amazing mama with an awesome sense of humor. I can always count on her to make me laugh and respond to my sarcasm with sarcasm!

The Gramma character is based on my aunt. However, he is much more than an aunt to me...she is one of my closest, special friends!

The Baby Mama character is based on my cousin. She is now a new and proud mama to a precious baby girl! I have yet to reflect this in my comics, but I will soon!

The Dollie Mama character is based on my friend Dollie! Yep! That is her real name! She has been a Comic Strip Mama fan since I started my venture. We started chatting on a personal level and we instantly bonded!

The Creelmama character is based on a fan who comments and shares her life with me on my page! She is hysterically hilarious!

The Wise Mama character is also based on a fan, Sandra Wise. She is a writer and an entrepreneur who has followed me and shared my work for a very long time!

Meet MY Real "Mama In Crime"!

©2013 Comic Strip Mama Enterprises Inc.

Cheryl Kaye Tardif is an International Bestselling Author and I'm proud to say that she is my "cousin-in-love" and my mentor!

Yes, this is a little bit of a promo, but she deserves it! She has worked extremely hard to achieve her success and she is a talented and incredible, mama, author, story teller and publisher. My words will never do her justice.

Cheryl, thank you from the bottom of my heart for being such an awesome role mole and for encouraging me and believing in me! You truly deserve all of your success!

If you haven't already, I strongly recommend that you read her works!

www.cherylktardif.com

Meet MY Lil' Anti-Bullying Buddies!

©2013 Comic Strip Mama Enterprises Inc.

I am a passionate anti-bullying advocate. AntiBULLYotics!™ is a division of the Comic Strip Mama Enterprises Inc. webcomic productions! Through comics and advocacy, AntiBULLYotics promotes awareness and provides a dose of intervention, prevention and rehabilitation for VICTIMS & BULLIES. I believe that the most important step in making positive changes and choices is encouraging victims and bullies to embrace their self-respect, self-worth and self-love in order to reinvent themselves into stronger, better people...In other words, every victim and bully should achieve awesomeness!

Comic Strip Kids™ is a brand new webcomic production venture that should be in full swing by the end of 2013!

Just Comics!
For Your Reading Pleasure!

Comic Strip Mama! ™
I need to find a career where my PAY is based solely on how AWESOME I AM!
Work is SO much WORK!
Laptop
comicstripmama.com
©2013 Comic Strip Mama Enterprises Inc.
services@comicstripmama.com

Comic Strip Mama! ™
I really wish that ONE of my personalities LOVED to CLEAN!
comicstripmama.com
©2013 Comic Strip Mama Enterprises Inc.

Comic Strip Mama! ™
Laptop
What IF we are ALL just characters in a great BIG book of LIFE and when we FORGET what we are going to DO or going to SAY, it's because the AUTHOR is BACKSPACING!
©2013 comicstripmama.com
©2013 Comic Strip Mama Enterprises Inc.

Comic Strip Mama! ™
I better GET UP and walk around before I get another classic case of LAPTOPITIS!
©2013 comicstripmama.com
©2013 Comic Strip Mama Enterprises Inc.

Comic Strip Mama! ™
I could tolerate HOT FLASHES a LOT better if they melted away some of my extra pounds instead of my SANITY!
©2013 comicstripmama.com
©2013 Comic Strip Mama Enterprises Inc.

Comic Strip Mama! ™
One good thing about my age... I made most of my stupid mistakes BEFORE the INTERNET!
Liquid SANITY!
Laptop
comicstripmama.com
©2013 Comic Strip Mama Enterprises Inc.

Comic Strip Mama! ™
I am NOT getting OLD... I am becoming VINTAGE!
©2013 comicstripmama.com
©2013 Comic Strip Mama Enterprises Inc.

Comic Strip Mama! ™
Sometimes I wish LIFE choices had an AUTOCORRECT FUNCTION!
©2013 comicstripmama.com

Comic Strip Mama! TM
Sweetie can you get me...
When I said "I DO"... I didn't mean EVERYTHING!
GET IT YOURSELF!
You tell him mama!
comicstripmama.com
©2013 Comic Strip Mama Enterprises Inc.

Comic Strip Mama! ™
Sometimes... I wish LIFE had an "ESCAPE" button!
©2013 comicstripmama.com
©2013 Comic Strip Mama Enterprises Inc.

Comic Strip Mama! ™
I must get up...
My CAFFEINE
needs ME!
YAWN
©2013 comicstripmama.com

Comic Strip Mama! ™
Before I've had my COFFEE, I am whatever the opposite of "BRIGHT EYED and BUSHY TAILED" is!!
COFFEE Mama's Special Blend
©2013 comicstripmama.com

Comic Strip Mama! ™
Liquid Sanity!
Deep down, I'm totally a MORNING PERSON! Like REALLY DEEP down at the bottom of my second cup of COFFEE!!
©2013 comicstripmama.com

Comic Strip Mama! TM
CAFFEINE LOADING!!
Please STAND BACK!
comicstripmama.com
©2013 Comic Strip Mama Enterprises Inc.

Comic Strip Mama! ™
Behind every successful morning is a substantial amount of CAFFEINE!
ROCKET FUEL
©2013 comicstripmama.com

Comic Strip Mama! ™
Here's a list of things I'd be HAPPY to do before I have my first cup of COFFEE!
COFFEE Mama's Special Blend
©2013 comicstripmama.com
©2013 Comic Strip Mama Enterprises Inc.

Comic Strip Mama! ™
I don't ALWAYS write a "HONEY DO" LIST... BUT when I DO, I realize pretty quickly that I'm probably just writing a "Nevermind, I'll just DO IT MYSELF" LIST!
YEEAP!!
HONEY DO
comicstripmama.com

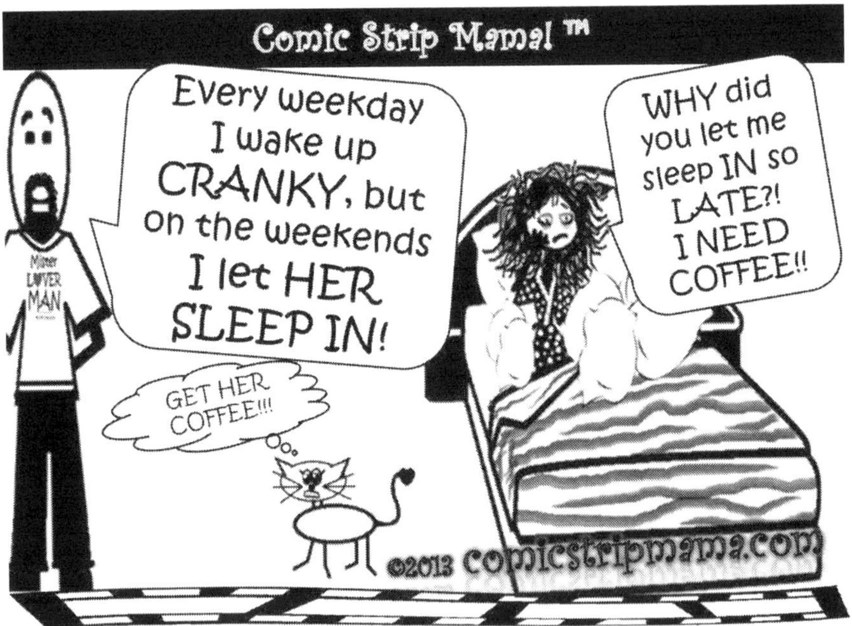

©2013 Comic Strip Mama Enterprises Inc.

Comic Strip Mama! ™
Ooooo YES! That was totally HOT! Say it AGAIN!!
Uhhhh... I did the dishes??
Yes! YES!!! Okay... Just say it ONE more time!!
Mister LOVER MAN
©2013 comicstripmama.com

Comic Strip Mama! ™
WINE is to WOMEN as DUCT TAPE is to MEN... It fixes EVERYTHING!!
Liquid FIX IT
comicstripmama.com
©2013 Comic Strip Mama Enterprises Inc.

Comic Strip Mama! ™
Liquid SANITY!
Ahhhhhhh... That AWESOME feeling when the first sip of WINE touches your SOUL and replenishes a few shreds of SANITY...
©2013 comicstripmama.com
©2013 Comic Strip Mama Enterprises Inc.

Comic Strip Mama! ™
Clinkity
Clink
So HE says to me... "It's ME or the WINE!!"... BAHAHAHA!! So anyway... CHEERS to the WEEKEND!!
comicstripmama.com
©2013 Comic Strip Mama Enterprises Inc.

Don't forget! My next book is going to be ALL about "the awesome, the insanity and the drama" of PARENTHOOD and being a MAMA!

Comic Strip Mama™

Being a MOM reminds us to be grateful for the simple things in life... Like sanity, sleep, spending money, eating a hot meal, taking a shower and peeing alone.

comicstripmama.com

©2013 Comic Strip Mama Enterprises Inc.

Official Comic Strip Mama™ Merchandise is now available!

Check out the shop at:
www.cafepress.com/comicstripmama

Make sure you visit the Comic Strip Mama™ website, subscribe to the blog and sign up for AWESOME email updates! Monthly fan giveaways and contests will start in September 2013! =)

www.comicstripmama.com

Follow me on Facebook and Twitter!
www.facebook.com/ComicStripMama
www.twitter.com/ComicStripMama

Thanks again for being awesome, for taking time to read this book and for laughing and sharing with me on my social media platforms! I wouldn't be doing what I love to do, if it wasn't for you! <3

Dedications & Special Mentions!

I will warn you that this section may be a *tad* long. It's not like excruciating long, but I'm pretty sure that it is a little bit longer than it should be. Cut me some slack, I'm a virgin author, this is my first book EVER and I have a lot of people to thank. It's actually kinda humorous and sweet. So do take a peek! =)

Oh, and...Try not to roll your eyes too much!

> Thank YOU!! THANK YOU!! I couldn't POSSIBLY thank you ENOUGH!!

©2013 Comic Strip Mama Enterprises Inc.

This book is dedicated with ALL my love, heart and soul to the following people for the following reasons:

To my amazing, wonderful, awesome children:
Joshua, Jamie & Alexis

Without you, my life as a Mama would not be possible. I am SO grateful for each one of you and I am so thankful for ALL of the joy, love, laughter, tears, mini heart-attacks, ER visits, challenges, grey hairs, chaos and INSANITY that each one of you have brought to my life in your own special way.

To my amazing, wonderful, awesome "Lover Man":
Kevin

Thank you for loving me, bringing out the best in me and believing in me despite my scatterbrain, and sometimes totally insane, ideas and ventures!

To my beautiful Daughters-In-Love:
Courtney & Alexis

Both of you are remarkable, kind, intelligent and adorable young women who should be very proud of the people you have become and everything you have accomplished in this life so far! Thank you for loving and caring for my baby boys.

To and in loving memory of my Mama & Father in Heaven:
Linda
May 22, 1953 — November 2, 1981
Raymond
December 5, 1951 — May 15, 2003

Thank you for giving me life. Not a day goes by that I don't think of you. I know that you are somehow still watching over and protecting me and my children. I feel it with every fibre of my being. I wish you were here to see this and I miss you like crazy!

OK… I'm almost done, I promise!

To my Love-Mama (aka: Step-Mama):
Cora

"You were born from my heart." I will never forget those words and I can't thank you enough for everything you have been, all that you have done and all the love you have given me because you wanted to.

To my Mama-In-Love and my Papa-In-Love:
Julia & Dan

Your kindness and generosity absolutely amazes me. I am so fortunate and grateful to have both of you in my life.

To some amazing Aunts and Uncles who believed in me, encouraged me

to be awesome and who went above and beyond their roles to save my bootie and help me through a lot of hard times in life, including:
Lisa & Roger, Pam & Guy, Greg & Helene, Nora & Dan

To my brothers & sister and their spouses: **Chris & Kelly, Ray & Stacey, Cathy & Jeff, "Bert" & Danielle**

To my Forever Friends!
Lisa, Maggie, Lisa, Sara, Pam

To my friend and main "Mama in Crime", **Dollie Phillips** (aka: Dollie Mama) who believed in my comic venture more than ANYONE else did and encouraged me every step of the way!

To my cousin-in-love and successful Best Selling International Author, **Cheryl Kaye Tardif** who has encouraged me, believed in my success and who has been an amazing mentor and friend.

And LAST, but certainly NOT LEAST:

To Rose, Peter, Linda, Michelle, Rob "Billy" and Jennifer at **Skebo & Associates** and to ALL of my **FAMILY** and **FRIENDS** who have believed in me and supported me throughout my comic journey, including my **Facebook READERS**!! YOU are the reason my dreams are coming true! There are no words that could properly thank you for your all of love and support and it would take an entire book to mention you all!!

About the Author

"Internet famous" for her humorous and inspirational self-syndicated webcomics about surviving the insanity of life and parenthood Tanya Masse, AKA: "Comic Strip Mama" is a mama, a writer, a cartoonist and an entrepreneur who has faced a tremendous amount of adversity throughout the challenges of her life and has risen above it all!

Through her comics, award winning blog, social media platforms and literary works, she entertains and encourages others to:

Make the best of the busyness, craziness, chaos, frustrations and challenges of life and parenthood!

Live on the AWESOME side!
STOP taking life SO SERIOUSLY!
Embrace the INSANITY!
Focus on the POSITIVE lessons!
Recognize the BLESSINGS!
Find the HUMOR whenever possible, and
CELEBRATE LIFE!

Connect with Comic Strip Mama at:

http://www.comicstripmama.com

http://www.facebook.com/ComicStripMama

http://www.twitter.com/ComicStripMama

IMAJIN BOOKS
Quality fiction beyond your wildest dreams

For your next eBook or paperback purchase, please visit:

www.imajinbooks.com

www.twitter.com/imajinbooks

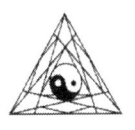

www.facebook.com/imajinbooks

Made in the USA
Charleston, SC
11 September 2013